Vege

Camp Without Coolers
18-Day Meal Plan

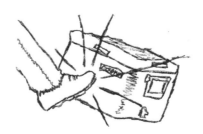

Kick the Cooler Habit!

Lacey Anderson

Thanks to my husband, Neil Nikirk, whose editing skill vastly improved this cookbook.

To my mother, Dianne Pabst, who spent countless hours hand-drawing the illustrations.

To my friend, Ben Webb, whose food photo graces the cover, taken on my favorite river – the Rio Maranon in Peru.

Please Review This Book on Amazon.com
If you like this book enough to award it four or five stars on Amazon.com, let everyone know. Your review can be as short or as long as you like. Once your review appears on Amazon.com, email Lacey using the contact form on her website www.nocoolers.com and she will send you a discount offer on other titles.

Text copyright © 2020 by Lacey Anderson
Cover design copyright © 2020 by Jamie Dalton of Magnetra's Design

This book is licensed for your personal enjoyment only. If you would like to share this book with another person, please purchase an additional copy for each person you share it with. Thank you for respecting the hard work of the author.

ISBN 978-0-9834093-8-0

TABLE OF CONTENTS

INTRODUCTION

This cookbook is a compilation of recipes and techniques from my three-booklet series titled Camp Without Coolers, Vegetarian. For this book, I have updated and compiled recipes from that series into a complete 18-day meal plan. This makes planning an extended river trip or other multi-week outdoor activity easier for you with all of the vegetarian recipes in one convenient place.

Every day includes recipes for breakfast, lunch, an appetizer, a main course, a side dish and a dessert; a complete meal plan for 18 days! If you are meal planning for less than 18 days, you can pick and choose individual recipes from the book to supplement your own camp recipe collection.

The recipes in this cookbook are perfect for the vegetarian rafter, kayaker, sea kayaker, and canoeist; in fact, they work well for all camping enthusiasts that prefer a plant-based diet and don't like lugging around a cooler full of ice. It also includes tips and techniques for the No Coolers kitchen and sources for some ingredients that may not be readily available at your local supermarket.

NO COOLERS TIPS

Repackaging at Home

Not All Plastic Bags are the Same.

If using plastic bags only use high quality reusable food storage plastic bags. These were hard to find when I wrote my first cookbook (over ten years ago), but now there are a variety of brands to choose from. Do a google search to find the myriad of products available, one is sure to be to your liking. Buy high-quality bags; generic or bargain-priced bags will not hold up to the rigors of the outdoor kitchen. Also note that some bags are fine to store food in, but not to place in boiling water. Be sure to read the directions and intended use for all plastic bags.

Repackage Before Your Trip

It is helpful to repackage all ingredients at home to cut down on the weight, bulk, and litter you will have to deal with while in the wilderness. Remember to always follow the Leave No Trace policies of "Pack It In, Pack It Out."

Following are the techniques: measure and mix together all dry ingredients for a recipe prior to the trip. Do not mix dry and wet or moist ingredients ahead of time. A vacuum sealer is handy if you have one. If you go this route, I recommend placing all of the ingredients for a meal into vacuum-sealed bags. This is great for river trips because it adds an extra waterproofing layer. These bags will need to be placed inside a dry bag or dry box while on the river. Do not depend on the vacuum sealed bags alone to keep your food dry when doing whitewater.

Be and Stay Organized

Organize repackaged ingredients into individual meal packets and then label the packets according to day and meal type. While on the trip maintain an organization system.

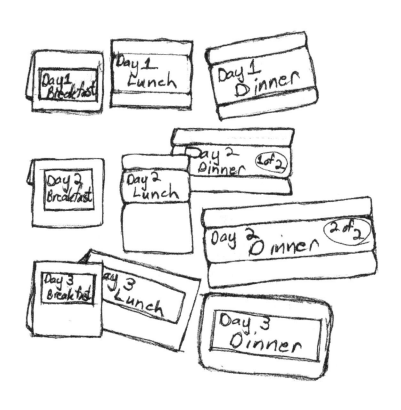

Commissary Kit and Recipe Book

The commissary kit is for foods that may leak if not bottled. This includes liquids, fats (stick margarine), and some powdery substances. Ingredients that are used frequently should be included in the commissary. In addition, special items that you do not want to put into the meal packets could go in the commissary.

Assembling a Commissary Kit

Repackage the Commissary items that may leak. Place these ingredients into secure containers (secure screw-top bottles meant for storing liquids without leakage when jostled or upside down). Label the containers clearly. You will want to be able to identify everything in the commissary kit.

Once you have all the individually labeled items, place them into one big container labeled Commissary Kit. Many different types of containers will work for a Commissary Kit. I suggest a small ammo can or a Vittle Vault*. I have also used dry bags

Recipe Book

In place of taking one of my cookbooks, photocopy the recipes and cooking directions. Then protect the photocopied pages inside a plastic bag. Place the plastic bag inside the commissary kit container.

*Vittle Vault: lightweight airtight storage container for packaged foods. With a spin of the patented lid, the Vittle Vault locks air and water tight. Made of high-impact-resistant plastic. Vittle Vaults are often used as pet food containers and can be found at most pet stores.

Appetizer and Dessert Every Day

I believe it is worth the extra effort to prepare appetizers and desserts. Don't worry about having to do more work because my recipes are so quick and easy to prepare you will not feel like a slave to the camp kitchen, but rather the happy and relaxed camp kitchen host.

After a day of activity, it is fantastic to pull into camp and immediately satisfy grumbling tummies with an appetizer. It puts a smile on people's faces and it tides them over until dinner. I often serve soup as an appetizer because the liquid helps to keep people hydrated. Some people have a tendency to not drink enough water, resulting in headaches and sometimes more serious health complications. With a tasty soup appetizer, I have the added security of knowing trip members are a bit more hydrated.

Desserts make a great end to a meal and provide extra calories for energy. Adding appetizers and desserts to dinner every day provides some entertainment and makes more food and calories available for individuals that need a little extra. The special touch of serving appetizers and desserts results in people realizing that the meal plan has been well thought out. It lets participants know they are being well taken care of.

The dinner entrée portions assume that appetizers and desserts will be served. If you choose to serve dinner without an appetizer or dessert you may want to adjust the main course recipes to produce a larger per-person portion; however, I do not recommend skipping the tasty appetizers and desserts.

Cheeses, "No Coolers" Style

Cheeses that are hard and contain less oils, fats and moisture will stay fresh the longest. If you want cheese to last, opt for a hard cheese such as Gruyere or aged Gouda which will last for a week or so. I have had good luck with string and mozzarella cheese, they seem to keep without a cooler for a week or so. I have had fresh Parmesan last for weeks without a cooler. The Kraft brand dried parmesan will last for several weeks.

The oils from some cheeses may separate leaving an oily film on the outside - this usually happens with softer cheeses. Enzymes and bacteria occur naturally in cheese and need to be exposed to air and moisture to keep the cheese fresh and flavorful. For this reason, fresh cheese should not be stored in an airtight wrapping, such as plastic wrap or a sandwich bag.

Wrap cheeses in wax or parchment paper, layers of cheesecloth or even a plain brown paper bag. Secure the wrapping and store the cheese in a cool container. Keep out of full sun, store in a cool spot, and keep cheese dry.

If your cheese begins to mold, you can salvage it. Make a cut about half inch below the mold to make sure it has been entirely removed and discard the moldy piece. The remaining cheese will be fine.

Canned cheese is also an option. Really, it is good! Bega is the brand I use and like very much, so much so that I keep it stocked in my home kitchen. Canned cheese can be ordered online, see the Recipe Ingredients Notes section for ordering information.

Freeze-dried vs Dehydrated (Dried)

Freeze-dried and dehydrated foods are very different from each other with very different cooking directions and preparation techniques. They are not normally interchangeable in recipes.

Freeze-dried

During the freeze-drying process, fresh produce is put into a large vacuum and brought to an extremely low temperature. A vacuum is applied and the moisture in the fruit is removed. This process allows for up to 97% of the liquid volume to be removed, much more than dehydrating. The end result is a product that is crisp and light with all of the nutritional value. Cell structure remains intact, which results in excellent retention of flavor, color, shape, and nutritional value.

Freeze-dried food can be eaten as is, or rehydrated. They are good for the quick meals because they rehydrate very quickly. They are good for recipes that do not require much cooking. Be careful, if freeze-dried items are cooked for too long, they may turn to mush.

Dehydrated (dried)

Dehydrated vegetables and fruits are made by subjecting vegetables and fruit to heat, resulting in water evaporation. When cooked, these vegetables rehydrate nicely and often remain intact. Dehydrated foods are better for the meals that require a longer cooking time because they maintain their form and texture even after a long simmer. In fact, if the dehydrated food does not cook long enough it may be tough or chewy.

Don't Get Kicked Out of the Tent!

A vegetarian and vegan diet has a lot of dietary fiber. Your body's digestive system may not be used to so much roughage. Many recipes contain an abundance of healthy complex carbohydrates. Some complex carbohydrates contain something called raffinose. Beans have a lot of it. Raffinose is also found in vegetables and whole grains.

Humans do not possess the enzyme in their stomach and upper intestine to easily digest the raffinose in these foods without producing gas. In the lower intestine, carbohydrates are fermented by gas-producing bacteria, which make methane, leading to the flatulence commonly associated with eating beans and other vegetables. The solution – Beano.

Beano is a natural enzyme dietary supplement that is used to help digest raffinose and reduce gas in the digestive tract, thereby preventing flatulence. It contains the enzyme alpha galactosidase that breaks down raffinose. It is available in both tablet and liquid form.

In order for Beano to be effective it needs to be consumed before eating your first bite. It prevents gas from happening; it will not stop the gas once you have it. For more information, see the Beano website: www.beanogas.com

INGREDIENT NOTES

The primary source for recipe ingredients will be your local supermarket, but international markets and health food stores can be excellent resources as well. Health food stores, in particular, are a good source of meatless entrees, grains, dairy substitutes, alternative noodles and more. Have fun exploring the shopping options in your neighborhood.

The ingredients for recipes in this cookbook are readily available in most regions of the USA, but some of the ingredients may be unfamiliar to you. Following are descriptions of some of the more unusual ingredients found in my recipes. Keep in mind, if you cannot find a product at your local grocer, almost all of the ingredients and food items can be ordered on Amazon.

Ancho Chili Powder – Ancho chili powder is made from dried Poblano chilies and has a milder, sweeter flavor than the American-style (New Mexico or California) chili powder. Look for ancho chili powder in the "International" aisle of your supermarket or at a local Mexican market (carneceria).

Bega Cheese Canned Cheddar Cheese – Bega brand is very good; I actually keep it in my home cupboard as well. It can be found online with a simple search, but the store Pleasant Hill Grain seems to have the best price for smaller orders. https://pleasanthillgrain.com/bega-canned-cheese-storable

Cacao and Cacao Nibs – Cacao is the pure form of chocolate; it is much less processed than cocoa powder or chocolate bars. Cacao beans are a product of the jungle; the tree grows in tropical environments, so the natural whole bean cacao can be hard to find in the USA. I have found whole cacao beans in the traditional mercados of South America. If you find these whole beans raw, roast the bean first, then crush into smaller pieces to use as a topping. Some USA specialty chocolate shops and health food stores carry Cacao Nibs. Beware, some nibs can have an excess of added sugar and little true cacao bean, read ingredient list.

Chayote is a type of squash native to the Americas. It grows profusely in Mexico and is common in USA markets. It is a small, hard and mild flavored squash that retains a bit of firmness even when cooked. It is a versatile vegetable that can be eaten raw, boiled, fried and added to any dish because it takes on the flavor of what it is cooked with.

Chia Seeds – These seeds are nutrient-dense and an excellent source of vitamins, antioxidants, protein, Omega-3 fatty acids, calcium, iron and more! This seed has become a staple in many households, thus more and more grocers are carrying them. This product can also be found in health food stores and larger supermarkets.

Crema – Crema is a delicious light cream. Find it in a can or small carton under the name Media Crema Table Cream. Most grocery stores stock it with the canned evaporated milk.

Dehydrated Shredded Potatoes (hash browns) – The key to success with dried potatoes is using shredded potatoes. I like the brand Hungry Jack Original Hash

Brown Potatoes. Most grocery stores carry them, look for them in a small square carton on a shelf, not in the refrigerated section. Honeyville brand is also good.

Dried Apples – (Dehydrated Apples) If you have a Trader Joe's store close by, I prefer that brand, but any brand should work. If there is not a Trader Joe's close to your house, you can order through Amazon.

Dried Peppers (Dehydrated Bell Pepper) – Harmony House Dehydrated Mixed Peppers are really good. I use them in all the recipes that call for dehydrated peppers. I keep them in my cupboard at home too.

English Cucumber – I usually purchase English cucumbers because they last longer than a traditional cucumber. I prefer the taste and texture. The seeds are smaller and the skin is thinner; you do not need to peel the skin. English Cucumbers are sometimes called seedless cucumbers. Find them wrapped in plastic in the grocery produce section.

Flatbread – This Middle Eastern style bread is reminiscent of a very thick flour tortilla. Flatout Flatbread is one of my favorite brands for its flavor and texture. This brand also stores well, it usually lasts for a week or so. Flour tortillas can be substituted for flatbread if you prefer.

Freeze-Dried Blueberries are so good they can be eaten by itself. Every brand I have tasted I enjoyed. Most of the nutrients are retained in the freeze-drying process so they make a healthy snack as well.

Freeze-Dried Corn is so good it can be eaten by itself. I have enjoyed every brand I have tasted. Most of the nutrients are retained in the freeze-drying process so it makes a healthy snack as well.

Freeze-Dried Raspberries – Contrary to what many people believe, the freeze-drying process actually maintains the nutritional value of foods. Here's how; the berries are placed on racks inside of a vacuum chamber. The temperature is lowered to below freezing and then slowly raised. The water in the berries moves from a solid state to a gaseous state which maintains the structure and nutritional value of the berries.

Hard Cheese – Most smoked and hard cheeses keep well without refrigeration. Look for cheeses with a lower fat content because they will keep better without a cooler. While the cheese is packed in the group food pack, take steps to keep the cheese as dry and as cool as possible. Try to keep it in shady spots, out of direct sunlight. Sometimes the oil will separate and give the cheese a wet surface, which bothers some people. To combat this, wrap the cheese in cheesecloth or some other very clean, absorbent material to soak up the moisture.

Hoisin Sauce is a sweet, spicy, dark red sauce made from soybeans, vinegar, sugar, garlic, and various spices, widely used in southern Chinese cooking.

Huancaina Sauce is a popular and traditional Peruvian sauce for potatoes. The common name is yellow hot chili cheese sauce. The homemade version is very basic, made from Aji peppers, fresh soft cheese and saltine crackers. The recipe in this cookbook uses a prepackaged sauce which is a product of Peru. It is very hard to find this sauce in USA grocery stores, but

Amazon has it. Order the brand Alacena; the name is Huancaina, but you may need to look for it under the full name, Crema de aji y queso Huancaina Receta Casera. It comes in a handy durable bag.

Hummus Powder (Dried) is so handy, I keep powdered hummus in my home cupboards as well. It is easy to mix a batch up whenever I like. The powdered variety is just as tasty as fresh! There are no worries with storing it for long periods of time in the dried state. It can be found in most supermarkets and health food stores. Fantastic Foods is my preferred brand.

Jicama - Also known as a Mexican potato. Jicama is a crunchy, juicy tuber that is often paired with chili powder, lemon, lime, oranges, ginger or even soy sauce. Eaten raw, simply peel, cut, slice or shred and add to salads, stir-fries or serve with dip. The small to medium sized jicamas have the best texture and flavor. If kept dry, Jicama keeps well for long periods of time.

Margarine, Stick – For the no cooler camp kitchen this is the best fat. I recommend using stick margarine because they last longer than margarine in a tub or butter.

Margarita Mix from Baja Bob's. The powdered margarita mix is fantastic! Some grocery stores and BevMo carry it. I like the "original" flavor the best. www.bajabob.com/

Napa Cabbage has oblong-shaped light green leaves with thick crisp stems and frilly ends. It has a mild flavor, a soft texture and is excellent eaten raw (or cooked). This Chinese cabbage is packed with antioxidants, vitamin C and dietary fiber. It keeps well without a cooler. Purchase compact, firm, crisp and fresh. There should be no brown spots on the ribs or wilted leaves.

NIDO (Dry Whole Milk Powder) – The key to good tasting powdered milk (like NIDO) is that it is made from whole milk, rather than skim or low-fat milk. NIDO can be found in many supermarkets and many international food stores.

Nut Butter – Individual packets are for the recipes called "Vegetarian Trail Lunch ~ Grab n Go" and the "Quick Trail Lunch". I prefer to distribute the individual packs of nut butters. As far as I know Justin's Nut Butters are the only company packaging as individual servings. The company also has different variety of butters, almond, cashew, etc.

Ova Easy Egg – Egg crystals are made with a revolutionary new technology that keeps the flavor and nutrition of fresh eggs intact. All they do is gently evaporate the water in the eggs... that's it. Egg crystals aren't cooked until you cook them!

Parmesan Cheese – If using perishable fresh cheeses, most smoked and hard cheeses keep well without refrigeration. Look for cheeses with a lower fat content. Aged parmesan cheeses that are hard and contain less oils, fats and moisture will stay fresh the longest without refrigeration or coolers. For my packing technique the cheese is packed in the group food pack, but take steps to keep fresh cheese as dry and as cool as possible (you may want to separate out). Try to keep it in shady spots, out of direct sunlight. Sometimes the oil will separate and give the cheese a wet surface, which bothers some people. To combat this, wrap the cheese in cheesecloth or some other very clean, absorbent material to soak up the moisture. For a much easier product to use in the no coolers kitchen, buy Kraft brand dried parmesan cheese. This product requires less special handling as it is semi-perishable (in fact, almost nonperishable), thus keeps better in the no coolers kitchen.

PB2 (Powdered Peanut Butter) – Peanuts are first roasted and then pressed to remove most of the fat and oil. The dried powder is a lightweight, nonperishable food. Just add water; voila, you have peanut butter!

Quinoa – Quinoa is an ancient seed used by the Incas. The Incas held the crop to be sacred. They referred to quinoa as the mother of all grains. Quinoa was of great nutritional importance in pre-Columbian Andean civilizations.

Quinoa Flakes – An almost instant Quinoa! Quinoa is a high protein grain with a slightly nutty flavor. Quinoa flakes are made from pressed quinoa, no more, no less.

Refried Beans (Instant) – These instant beans are convenient, consistent and time-saving, they have no cholesterol, no preservatives and are rich in protein and iron. Mexicali Rose is my favorite brand as there is no "canned taste." Their humorous slogan is "Kick the Can" and my no coolers slogan is "Kick the Cooler Habit"!

Rice (white, brown, parboiled, instant). – Rice is a versatile staple and is always available in many varieties. Instant rice cooks the fastest and mixes with everything.

Sesame Oil – This oil has a unique flavor that adds to the aroma and flavor of dishes, especially Asian foods. Sesame oil also has a high smoke point, making it good for frying foods.

Shallots are basically small onions. For recipes with a serving size of 4, I find that regular onions are usually too big. I normally want a smaller portion of chopped onions, but I do not like throwing out half an onion. So, I have found that shallots are a better size and work as an excellent replacement for traditional onions.

Soba Noodles – Soba is a Japanese word for buckwheat. Buckwheat soba noodles have a nutty full-bodied flavor. If you desire the traditional soba noodles check the ingredient list for buckwheat, as some brands add wheat or are even all wheat. I like all the varieties, wheat or buckwheat.

Sun Dried Tomatoes – In my opinion California Sun Dry brand is the best. This brand has a pleasing moist and fresh texture with a rich tomato flavor. Other brands can be too salty. I recommend the tomatoes that are packed with herbs and are in a glass jar. If you do not want to pack with glass then they make a product in plastic packaging as well.

Tahini – A paste made from toasted sesame seeds that is highly nutritious. Buy it in small quantities for the "Camp Without Coolers" kitchen because once the container is opened, it needs to be completely eaten or kept refrigerated due to the high oil content. Mighty Sesame Co, Fine Sesame Tahini is my favorite brand.

Tasty Bites – These are healthy, instant, pre-packaged meal toppers for rice. All varieties are inspired by

Indian food. They come in handy pouches and are healthy and flavorful. I enjoy most of the varieties, but my favorite is "Bombay Potatoes." Check out the ingredient list: potatoes, chickpeas, tomatoes, onions, sunflower oil, salt, ginger, garlic, coriander, chilies, cumin, and spices. That's it, simple. No unhealthy ingredients, chemicals, or food dyes.

Your local store may not carry the brand "Tasty Bites" but there are several different brands that are just as tasty. It's good to experiment at home first for your particular dietary needs and palate.

Tofu, shelf-stable UHT boxed – Choose an extra-firm tofu with an expiration date well into the future. The date is often a better indicator of quality than the brand. That being said, I have been very happy with the taste and texture of Mori-Nu brand.

Tostados, Mexican – the best ones for the no coolers kitchen come in a box with sturdier packaging so for a river trip they are a great choice. Then when they are served people can break them into piece sizes desired.

True Lemon and Lime – A 100% natural product; it is made from lemons and limes. Cold pressing and crystallizing the lemons locks in the great flavor and nutrients.

TVP (Taco Flavored) – Texturized vegetable protein (TVP) is a "soy meat." The soy beans provide protein, fiber, vitamins, and calcium. TVP is low in fat and cholesterol and has few calories.

Ultra Gel is an instant, gluten-free product that is used for thickening cold or hot dishes. It is made from waxy maize (corn).

Add your own ingredient notes:

_____

_____

_____

_____

_____

_____

_____

_____

_____

_____

_____

_____

_____

_____

_____

_____

_____

_____

_____

_____

_____

_____

_____

On-line Sources for Dehydrated and Freeze-Dried Products:

> Honeyville:
> http://honeyville.com/
>
> North Bay Trading:
> http://www.northbaytrading.com/
>
> Frontier Coop:
> http://www.frontiercoop.com/
>
> Harmony House:
> http://www.harmonyhousefoods.com/
>
> Amazon:
> http://www.amazon.com/

MEAL PLAN

This cookbook is divided into 3 parts – each corresponding to consecutive 6-day periods, providing a complete meal plan for 18 days! Every day includes breakfast, lunch, appetizer, main course, side dish and dessert. I've included a section on happy hour cocktails.

In the no coolers kitchen, it is very important to pay attention to the ingredients in each recipe and which day of the 18-day meal plan to serve them. Recipes for use during the first 6 days are predominantly fresh produce and have ingredients that are perishable. These items will not last longer than about a week without ice/cooler. The second 6 days of the meal plan includes recipes that use semi-perishable produce, canned goods and dried food items. The majority of recipes in the third 6 days of the meal plan use longer-lasting produce and dehydrated and/or freeze-dried ingredients.

Follow my meal plan and use the recipes in the order suggested and you will be able to eat well for 18 days, yet have your food pack be lightweight and cooler free! You can change the order of meals within each 6-day period to suit your taste but DO NOT swap recipes between the suggested 6-day periods. My suggestions for days 6, 12 and 18 are super-fast and easy recipes. I prefer to have at least one day per week with very little cooking; these are my go-to recipes for fast and easy camp cooking!

Go out enjoy nature, spend social time with friends and family or just relax. There is no need to slave away in the camp kitchen with my recipes!

Days 1 to 6: Fresh & Healthy

Important Note: The ingredients in the recipes for the first 6 days need to be used during the first week of an 18-day journey because they are perishable or semi-perishable food items.

DAY 1

Breakfast: Fresh Breakfast Buffet

Lunch: Avocado Pita Buffet

Dinner:

> Appetizer: Hummus Dip for Veggies and Chips
>
> Main Course: Red Coconut Curry
>
> Side Dish: Basic Rice
>
> Dessert: No-Bake Peanut Butter Chocolate Bars

DAY 2

Breakfast: Breakfast of the Incas

Lunch: Buckwheat Soba Noodles with Veggies

Dinner:

> Appetizer: Guacamole with Tortilla Chips
>
> Main Course: North African Couscous with Harissa
>
> Side Dish: Homemade Garlic Naan
>
> Dessert: Key Lime Dessert de Veracruz

DAY 3

Breakfast: Southwest Tofu Breakfast Burritos

Lunch: Cabbage Wraps with Peanut Sauce

Dinner:

> Appetizer: Instant Hot and Sour Soup
>
> Main Course: Chop Suey de Peru with Basic Rice
>
> Side Dish: Crunchy Salt Cured Tofu
>
> Dessert: Homemade Fudge with Strawberries

DAY 4

Breakfast: Quick Apple Quinoa

Lunch: Pasta de Peru

Dinner:

> Appetizer: PB2 Dipping Sauce with Veggies
>
> Main Course: Hearty Lentil Vegetable Stew
>
> Side Dish: Colorful Carrot Slaw
>
> Dessert: Raspberry No-Bake Cheesecake

DAY 5

Breakfast: Raspberry Chocolate Pancakes

Lunch: Vegan Aztec Tostadas

Dinner:

> <u>Appetizer:</u> Popcorn
>
> <u>Main Course:</u> Falafel with Tahini and Cucumber Sauces
>
> <u>Side Dish:</u> Creamy Cabbage Slaw and Asian Quinoa
>
> <u>Dessert:</u> No-Bake Coconut Chocolate Cookies

DAY 6

Breakfast: Fresh Breakfast Buffet

Lunch: Trail Lunch

Dinner:

> <u>Appetizer:</u> Soup
>
> <u>Main Course:</u> Tasty Bites with Rice
>
> <u>Side Dish:</u> Super-Fast Lentils
>
> <u>Dessert:</u> Royal Dansk Butter Cookies

Days 7 to 12: Quick & Easy

Important Note: The ingredients in the recipes for days 7 through 12 will last into the second week of an 18-day journey but need to be eaten during this week because they have a limited shelf life which include semi-perishable fresh items, canned goods and dried items.

DAY 7

Breakfast: Breakfast Buffet

Lunch: Tomato Hummus Lime Wraps

Dinner:

<u>Appetizer:</u> Veggies with Peanut Dipping Sauce

<u>Main Course:</u> Hoisin Tofu Stir Fry

<u>Side Dish:</u> Garlic Brown Rice

<u>Dessert:</u> Chocolate Sea Salt Almonds

DAY 8

Breakfast: Marley's Apple Pancakes

Lunch: Ginger Soba Noodle Salad

Dinner:

<u>Appetizer:</u> Guacamole with Tortilla Chips

<u>Main Course:</u> Vegetarian Burrito Bar

<u>Side Dish:</u> Tex-Mex Rice

<u>Dessert:</u> Ginger Tea with Pineapple Slices

DAY 9

Breakfast: Vegetarian Breakfast Burrito

Lunch: Quick Trail Lunch (or Tahini Spread) & GORP

Dinner:

>Appetizer: Instant Soup
>
>Main Course:
>
>>Sweet and Spicy Thai Noodles
>>
>>Crunchy Salt-cured Tofu
>
>Side Dish: Creamy Carrot Slaw
>
>Dessert: Nut Fudge

DAY 10

Breakfast: Guatemalan Mosh with Eliza's Platanos

Lunch: Terra's Lunch Couscous

Dinner:

>Appetizer: Popcorn
>
>Main Course: Dreamy Sauce Pasta
>
>Side Dish:
>
>>Sweet and Sour Fruit Salad
>>
>>Garlic Bread
>
>Dessert: S'more Rice Krispie Treats

DAY 11

Breakfast: Date Couscous

Lunch: Cowboy Caviar

Dinner:

> <u>Appetizer:</u> Pesto Rounds
>
> <u>Main Course:</u> Papas a la Huancaina con Arroz
>
> <u>Side Dish:</u> Southwest Quinoa
>
> <u>Dessert:</u> Chocolate Walnuts

DAY 12

Breakfast: Breakfast Buffet

Lunch: Quick Trail Lunch and GORP

Dinner:

> <u>Appetizer:</u> Instant Soup
>
> <u>Main Course:</u> Spaghetti in Marinara Sauce
>
> <u>Side Dish:</u> Chayotes Fritos
>
> <u>Dessert:</u> Royal Dansk Butter Cookies

Days 13 to 18: Effortless & Carefree

Important Note: The ingredients in the recipes for days 13 through 18 will last into the third week of an 18-Day journey because they are nonperishable, being longer-lasting vegetables, freeze-dried, dried and canned items.

DAY 13

Breakfast: Breakfast Buffet for Nomads

Lunch: Trail Lunch for Nomads and GORP

Dinner

>   Appetizer: Mexico Jicama Sticks
>
>   Main Course: Marley's South of the Border Burritos
>
>   Side Dish: Mexican Chayote
>
>   Dessert: Rum Balls

DAY 14

Breakfast: Fast Blueberry Quinoa

Lunch: Italian Couscous Buffet &

Dinner

>   Appetizer: Tahini Spread
>
>   Main Course: Sweet Potato Quinoa Buffet
>
>   Side Dish: Crunchy Garlic Tofu
>
>   Dessert: Chocolate Coconut Balls

DAY 15

Breakfast: Western Scramble with Spiced Hot Apples

Lunch: Eastern Hummus Wraps

Dinner

> Appetizer: Corn and Pepper Soup
>
> Main Course: Vegetarian Tacos for Nomads
>
> Side Dish: Spanish Rice for Nomads
>
> Dessert: Chocolate Chia Pudding

DAY 16

Breakfast: Quinoa de Canela

Lunch: Black Bean Corn Salad

Dinner

> Appetizer: Popcorn
>
> Main Course: Tamarindo Fried Rice
>
> Side Dish: Fried Platanos
>
> Dessert: Mud Cookies

DAY 17

Breakfast: River Ranger Oats

Lunch: Quinoa Tabouli

Dinner

Appetizer: Popcorn

Main Course: Potato Corn Chowder

Side Dish: Garlic Naan

Dessert: Chocolate PB Medjools

DAY 18

Breakfast: Breakfast Buffet for Nomads

Lunch: Trail Lunch for Nomads

Dinner

Appetizer: Instant Soup

Main Course: Creamy Lemony Pasta

Side Dish: Creamed Chayote

Dessert: Royal Dansk Butter Cookies

~~~~~~~~~~~~~~~~~~~~~~~~~~~~~~~~~~~~~

WEEK 1
DAYS 1 TO 6

~ FRESH & HEALTHY ~

It is important to use the recipes in this first section during the first 6 days of a long trip.

The recipes in this first section are meant to be used in the first 6 days because they are made with ingredients that are either semi-perishable or perishable.

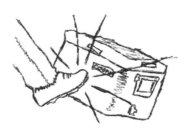

Kick the Cooler Habit!

~~~~~~~~~~~~~~~~~~~~~~~~~~~~~~~~~~~~~

BREAKFAST ~ DAYS 1 TO 6

Breakfast of the Incas

The original Superfood; packed with lots of nutrition. This porridge is wonderful served with a local fresh fruit; my favorite choices are bananas and mangoes.

4 Servings

> 3 ½ cups water
>
> ¾ cup quinoa
>
> ¾ cup oatmeal
>
> ¼ cup sunflower seeds (raw is best) or pumpkin seeds or mixture of the two
>
> 2 tablespoons chia seeds
>
> 1 tablespoon sesame seed

Serve with:

> Cacao Nibs or pure Cacao beans (see Ingredient Notes section of cookbook)
>
> 1 large mango
>
> 1 banana
>
> 1 papaya
>
> 3 tablespoon dry whole milk powder (NIDO)
>
> 1 cup water (to reconstitute milk)
>
> Sweeteners, honey, sugar, etc.

Rinse the quinoa first, a cheesecloth works well. Add the quinoa and water to a large pot, bring to a boil, cover. Turn down flame and simmer the quinoa for about 15 minutes. Add oatmeal and cook a few minutes more. Remove from flame, add seeds, stir and set aside.

Cut the fruit into bite sized chunks, set aside. Reconstitute the milk powder, set aside. Prepare the Cacao. If you found fresh roasted cacao beans, crush them and set aside. If it is cacao nibs you are using, place them in a bowl and set aside.

To Serve: set out the quinoa-oatmeal porridge, the fresh fruit, the cacao, the milk and the sweeteners buffet style. Each person makes their custom porridge mix.

Variation: be creative, add more quinoa, or oatmeal. Add nuts instead of seeds. Adjust the proportions of oatmeal to quinoa to your taste. Also adjust the amount of water dependent upon how thick or thin you prefer the porridge. The possibility in variety is endless, determined by the cook's palate.

Southwest Tofu Breakfast Burritos

A delicious and filling way to start the day. Two skillets work best, one for the hardy potatoes and the second for carefully cooking the tofu and veggies.

4 servings

> 1 (16 ounce) box extra firm tofu
>
> 1 sweet potato
>
> ½ to ¾ cup olive oil
>
> ½ onion, diced
>
> ½ red bell pepper, diced
>
> 1 cup kale, chopped (optional)
>
> 1 teaspoon salt
>
> 1 teaspoon garlic powder
>
> 1 teaspoon cumin
>
> ½ teaspoon ancho chili powder
>
> 6 flour tortillas, large burrito sized

On the Side:

> Salsa
>
> Tabasco

Tofu: pat tofu dry and wrap in a clean, absorbent towel. Place something heavy on top, such as a cast iron skillet, for 15 minutes or more. This process is to squeeze / press out as much liquid as possible.

Sweet Potatoes: dice the sweet potato into small cubes (no larger than ½ inch). Start with about ¼ cup oil to sauté potatoes, add a bit more if needed.

34

Sauce: while tofu is draining and potatoes are frying, prepare sauce by adding salt, garlic powder, cumin and ancho chili powder to a small bowl. Add enough water to make a pourable sauce. Set aside.

Peppers and Onions: chop peppers and onions. Warm oil in a second skillet. Start with about ¼ cup oil to sauté, add a bit more oil if needed. When oil is hot, add peppers and onion. Cook until softened, about 3 minutes. Add (optional) kale to peppers and onions, cover to steam for about 2 minutes. Kale is optional, but it is surprisingly good in this dish and adds vitamins.

In the meantime, unwrap tofu and use a fork to crumble into bite-sized pieces.

Use a spatula to move the onions and peppers to one side of the pan and add tofu. Sauté for 2 minutes, then add sauce. Stir immediately, evenly distributing the sauce. Cook for another 5 to 7 minutes until tofu is slightly browned.

To Serve: warm flour tortillas over flame. Fill tortillas with a couple scoops of the tofu, pepper, onion, kale and sauce scramble. Individual diners can add a dollop of sweet potatoes, splash of salsa and tabasco to taste. Roll like a burrito and chow down – Yum!

Raspberry Chocolate Pancakes

Chocolate and raspberry, the perfect flavor combination. And who doesn't like pancakes on a camping trip?

Yields 12 (3-inch diameter) pancakes

Raspberry Syrup

     1 ½ cups freeze-dried raspberries

     2 cups water

     ½ cup sugar

     2 tablespoons Ultra Gel

     1 teaspoon lemon juice

Pancakes

     2 cups Bisquick mix

     2 tablespoons dry whole milk powder (NIDO)

     2 tablespoons sugar

     3 to 4 tablespoons coconut oil

     1 ½ cup water

     1 small jar Nutella

Make the Raspberry Syrup First: add raspberries, water and sugar to a boil, turn to low, and simmer for about a minute. Remove from flame and add Ultra Gel to thicken.

Pancakes: add Bisquick, milk powder and sugar to a bowl, stir. Add 2 tablespoons of coconut oil and blend with fork to make little crumb like texture. Add water and stir to blend.

Place remaining coconut oil in fry pan or griddle and heat oil. Pour pancake mixture onto griddle, making the cakes, cook until bubbles form, flip, and cook till they are a golden brown.

To Serve: drop a teaspoon or so of Nutella onto pancake, spread Nutella and then pour a splash of raspberry syrup over pancake.

Fresh Breakfast Buffet

If food shopping in a region with fresh tropical fruit or berries include them in the fresh breakfast buffet for a local flair.

4 Servings

   ½ pound granola (2 cups) or cereal of choice

   1 cup nuts of choice

   1 cup dried fruits (raisins, craisins, dates or figs)

   2 tablespoons chia seeds

   ¼ cup Cacao Nibs or pure Cacao beans, crushed (see Ingredients Notes section of cookbook)

   ¾ quart soy or nut milk, boxed

   ½ quart soy yogurt (optional)

   4 apples or oranges

   8 breakfast or energy bars

   4 muffins or other breakfast bread of choice

Cut the tropical fruit into bite-size pieces; leave apples and oranges whole. Serve everything buffet style.

Each person takes a piece of fruit and energy bar. If they do not eat it for breakfast, have it for a snack later.

When everyone is done eating breakfast distribute the leftovers between the group to be consumed as snacks throughout the day.

Quick Apple Quinoa

Quinoa Flakes are fast to cook, an almost instant quinoa!

4 Servings

>   3 apples, cored and diced
>
>   2 ½ cups apple juice
>
>   ¼ cup coconut oil
>
>   2 cups Quinoa Flakes
>
>   ½ cup instant oatmeal
>
>   ½ cup raisins or other dried fruit
>
>   3 tablespoons honey
>
>   Pinch of salt
>
>   Cinnamon, on side

Use a thick bottomed pot.

Peel, core and dice the fresh apples. Place the fresh apple and the raisins in the pot with a pinch of salt and cook apples until soft, about 5 minutes. Add coconut oil to fruit and stir.

Slowly mix in the quinoa and oatmeal, it should be a bit watery. Add water a couple of tablespoons at a time if it needs to be thinner. On lowest heat, cook for 2 minutes. Maintain the quinoa in a thinner consistency for these 2 minutes. Watch it closely, adding more water if needed.

Add honey, remove from flame and let sit, with lid on, for 5 minutes. Serve the cinnamon on the side for topping.

LUNCH ~ DAYS 1 TO 6

Days 1 to 6: Fresh & Healthy – use the following recipes during the first 6 days of a long trip.

Avocado Pita Buffet

A variation on one of my favorite vegetarian sandwiches.

4 Servings

> 4 whole pita pockets
>
> 1 cup stuffed olives, sliced
>
> 4 medium avocados
>
> 3 tomatoes, sliced
>
> 8 ounces string cheese
>
> 1 head of romaine lettuce
>
> Mustard
>
> Mayonnaise

Slice the tomatoes, avocados, and olives. Pull apart the cheese and lettuce.

To Serve: lay everything out buffet style and let people make their own sandwiches.

Buckwheat Soba Noodles & Veggies

Mix and match a variety of vegetables to suit your palette.

4 Servings

>   1 (8 ounce) package buckwheat soba noodles
>
>   ⅓ cup unseasoned rice vinegar (lighter, sweeter flavor than other vinegars)
>
>   ⅓ cup vegetable oil
>
>   1 tablespoon olive oil
>
>   1 tablespoon Sriracha Hot Chili Sauce
>
>   1 ½ pounds (about 8 cups or more) mixed vegetables cut into matchstick-size pieces (suggest 3 carrots, 4 radishes, 1 English cucumber, 1 red or yellow bell pepper)
>
>   1 cup cilantro leaves with tender stems
>
>   2 scallions, thinly sliced
>
>   1 tablespoon sesame seeds
>
>   Salt and Pepper to taste

Morning Prep: cook noodles in morning. Follow package directions. Once done place the noodles in a secure package to store for the day.

Lunchtime Prep: in a large bowl, whisk vinegar, oils, and hot chili sauce completely, to emulsify. Add noodles, carrots, radishes, cucumber and bell pepper, toss to coat. Season with salt and pepper. Add cilantro and scallions. Toss in sesame seeds and serve. Set out the bottle of Sriracha hot chili sauce and extra rice vinegar on side for people who like it spicy!

Cabbage Wraps with Peanut Sauce

A friend that lives full-time on her sailboat enjoys preparing this recipe for boat guests. She doubles the delectable peanut sauce amount and serves it as a dip.

Yields 2 cups of dip

Peanut Sauce

> 1 cup crunchy peanut butter (unsweetened)
>
> ⅔ cup orange juice (about 1 ½ fresh oranges)
>
> 5 cloves garlic, minced
>
> 2 tablespoons soy sauce
>
> 2 tablespoons brown sugar
>
> 2 tablespoons water (or a little more)
>
> ½ teaspoon red pepper flakes, add more for spicier flavor

Filling – 4 Servings

> 1 red onion
>
> 2 red peppers
>
> 1 small jicama
>
> 2 carrots
>
> 1 English cucumber
>
> 1 (12 ounce) box tofu, boxed UHT extra firm (optional, but tasty!)

Wrap

> 1 head Napa cabbage*

Morning Prep: follow these directions for the tofu slices to have a delicious crispy crust. Open the package, drain out the water, and cut tofu into slabs about 3/8" thick, then cut those into thirds long ways. That will give you a nice ratio of crust to interior when frying. Next, place the tofu in a large bowl and bring some well-salted water to a boil. Carefully pour the hot water over your tofu. Let this stand for about 15 minutes, then drain.

Next, carefully lay the tofu strips out in a single layer on a clean cotton dishtowel. Put another clean dishtowel on top and gently pat, all over, to remove as much surface moisture as possible. This is going to allow for a "dry" tofu that will brown when fried. It will also reduce unpleasant sputtering of hot oil while cooking.

Heat a flat-bottomed skillet over high heat. When hot, add about 2 tablespoons of coconut, canola or virgin olive oil (only use an oil with a high smoke point). Swirl to cover the surface. Pat the tofu dry one more time and put it in the hot skillet it in a single layer, with plenty of room around each piece. Don't crowd the pan, or the heat will drop too much and the tofu will steam, not brown. Cook on one side until it is deeply golden brown, then flip. When both sides are done, remove to a plate and season with a little salt. Let cool completely and set in a safe place until lunch time.

The key to cooking tofu for these wraps is to get the tofu really dry, fry it in a hot skillet with a thin layer of oil on the bottom of the pan, don't crowd the pan, and cook it until the tofu strips are a golden brown.

Lunchtime Prep: mix all the ingredients for the peanut sauce and set aside.

Chop the red onion, red peppers, jicama, carrots and English cucumber into matchstick shaped and sized pieces. Pull apart the leaves of cabbage. Set out all of the vegetables on a platter. Let each person make their own wraps by placing the chopped veggies and tofu on a cabbage leaf, pouring some peanut sauce into the leaf and rolling. You can also have some extra peanut sauce on the side for dipping.

*Napa Cabbage has a more delicate texture and milder flavor than green or red cabbage, making it perfect for eating raw. It has a distinctive barrel-shape with a thick white rib and crisp, pale green, tightly-wrapped leaves. The leaves are large enough and shaped well for use as a bread substitute. It will stay fresh for a few weeks without a cooler if cared for properly; kept out of the sun and extreme heat. Best to leave the heads whole and don't wash or cut them until you're ready to prep. Napa cabbage is also loaded with vitamins, especially vitamin C. Some nutrition experts claim it to one of the healthiest vegetables around.

Variation: in place of the cabbage for a wrap you can use a variety of products such as soft tortillas, thin flatbread, etc. Use your imagination or maybe you already have a favorite wrap? There is a product I really like it is called Spring Rolls Skin which is made from tapioca and rice starch. There are several different brands. If you use this please follow the directions on the package for rehydrating as there are variances.

Pasta de Peru

I acquired this recipe from a native river guide I worked alongside on the Rio Maranon, aka "The Grand Canyon of the Amazon," in the Andes and jungle of northern Peru.

4 Servings

½ onion, small (red is my preference)

2 carrots

1 celery stalk

¼ cup white vinegar

¼ teaspoon garlic powder

1 (16 ounce) package macaroni

8 eggs (optional)

¾ cup parmesan cheese (fresh is best, but Kraft will work too)

¾ cup mayonnaise

¾ tablespoon mustard

¼ teaspoon salt

¼ teaspoon pepper

Morning Prep: cook the macaroni in the morning and hard boil 8 eggs. Once done place the noodles and eggs in a secure package to store for the day.

Lunchtime Prep: finely chop the celery and carrots, grate the cheese if needed. Mix the macaroni, vegetables, cheese, and condiments. Peel hard boiled eggs, slice thick and gently toss in the macaroni salad.

Vegan Aztec Tostadas

Cool dish for hot summer evenings; a great summer time dish when it is just "too hot to be in the kitchen".

4 Servings

    1 (15 ounce) can corn

    1 (15 ounce) can black beans

    1 (7 ounce) can green salsa

    1 (4 ounce) can mild green chilies

    ½ teaspoon ancho chili powder (optional)

    1 carrot

    1 lime

    ½ Green cabbage, small head

    1 bag hard tostada shells

    1 can small crema

    1 can jalapeno chilies

Peel and grate the carrot and place in a bowl. Slice the cabbage into very thin slivers, add to carrots and squeeze lime juice over mixture. Pour 1 or 2 tablespoons of crema into the slaw, toss and set aside.

Drain the corn, beans, and green chilies. Mix the canned corn, black beans, and peppers in a small bowl (add just enough salsa to moisten) toss gently and set aside.

Set-out tostadas for a self-serve tostada bar. First layer is bean mixture, next layer is slaw. Top with crema, salsa, and jalapenos as desired.

Trail Lunch

This is my go-to lunch for a day when hiking is planned, or when people want to keep being active (hiking, boating, climbing, etc.) or when your group simply does not want to stop and take the time to set-up tables and such for a traditional group picnic.

I often set-up the buffet in the morning so that people can pack early and eat lunch whenever they choose throughout the day.

4 Servings

> 8 ounces smoked gouda, parmesan, or other hard cheese (see Ingredient Notes section of cookbook)
>
> 1 (8 ounce) jar peanut butter
>
> 1 (8 ounce) jar Nutella or other chocolate nut spread
>
> 1 (13 ounce) box of crackers (your choice)
>
> 6 ounces dried fruit
>
> 5 ounces nuts of your choice
>
> 8 apples
>
> 8 energy or granola bars
>
> 1 (10 ounce) package cookies (optional)
>
> 4 baggies or container for each person

Slice cheese, if necessary. Arrange all ingredients buffet style.

Hand out the individual baggies/containers so that each guest can assemble their own lunch.

HAPPY HOUR DRINKS

These drinks will work well on any day of your trip

During the early evening hours, mix up a few drinks,
set out a plate of appetizers and call out,

"Happy Hour!"

Then watch hungry, smiling guests, family and friends
come running to have a taste.

Margarita Time!

Tequila

Use only the highest quality (usually more expensive) tequila for sipping and shots; margaritas can be made with almost any quality and variety of tequila.

Silver (or Blanco) tequila is un-aged and has a strong agave flavor; it is usually clear. Reposado ("restful") tequila is aged in oak barrels from 2 months to a year; the color is usually golden. Anejos are aged in oak barrels for over a year (2 years for double anejo) giving a light brown color and more complex taste.

My favorite sipping tequilas (you can see I like anejos):

Seleccion 1146 anejo

Pueblo Viejo Orgullo anejo

El Diamante Del Cielo anejo - extremely tasty, if you can find it send me a bottle!

Gran Centenario anejo - a reasonably-priced, yet very good anejo

Sauza Conmemorativo anejo

Margaritas

Margaritas can be made with any tequila but "top shelf" margaritas usually use a quality reposado or anejo; however, a good silver can make a fantastic margarita. Costco (Kirkland) silver is pretty good for sipping and makes great margaritas. Sauza Hornitos also makes good margaritas. I am not a fan of Cuervo Gold or really cheap tequilas, even in my margaritas.

Simply Tasty Margarita

1 Serving

> 3 ounces Simply Limeade
>
> 1 to 1.5 ounces tequila
>
> Juice of 1 or 2 fresh limes.
>
> Coarse salt for rimming the drinking glass

This recipe is so easy and tasty it is my go-to recipe at home. Mix or shake and serve over ice. It's really good with a bit of salt on the rim of your drinking glass.

Neil's Authentic Margarita

A less sweet and more authentic Mexican margarita uses 3 parts fresh lime juice to 1-part tequila. Use agave nectar to sweeten to your taste.

Baja Bob's Sugar-Free Margarita

For an easy lightweight and non-perishable recipe, pack some of Baja Bob's sugar-free margarita mix (powder), mix it with water in camp, and follow the Simply Tasty Margarita recipe above using the mix instead of Limeade. If you don't have fresh limes, add a little True Lime powder to improve the flavor by adding tartness.

Pina Colada

I have had good canned varieties (there are a lot to choose from on the market). For canned Pina Coladas, simply pour the canned Pina Colada mix into a container and add the amount of rum you like. You can also experiment with canned coconut milk, pineapple juice, and rum.

Wine

Everyone has their own favorites, from boxes to aged vintages. Most brands come in glass containers. I do not recommend taking glass containers on an inflatable raft; you may want to pour the contents into a plastic bottle. To solve this problem, I often just purchase and take boxed wine.

APPETIZERS ~ DAYS 1 TO 6

Days 1 to 6: Fresh & Healthy – use the following recipes during the first 6 days of a long trip.

Hummus Dip for Vegetables & Chips

Powdered hummus is an amazing kitchen item for the vegetarian following a no coolers philosophy. It is easy to prepare, tasty, nutritious and non-perishable. Did you know that hummus is made from chickpeas (garbanzo beans) which are high in protein, perfect for a vegetarian or vegan!

4 Servings

> 1 ½ cups hummus mix (dry powder)
>
> 1 ½ cups water (approximate)
>
> 2 tablespoons olive oil
>
> 1 lemon or lime (optional)
>
> 1 large bag of chips of choice
>
> 2 cups fresh veggies of choice

Place hummus mix in a bowl. Add 1 cup of water and the olive oil to mix, slowly add more water until it is the preferred consistency. For a zestier flavor add lemon or lime juice. Let set for 5 minutes.

Serve hummus as a dip for chips or fresh veggies such as carrots, jicama or red bell peppers for variety.

Guacamole with Tortilla Chips

As a kid growing up in the Mediterranean climate of east LA, we had a huge, and very productive, avocado tree in our backyard. I have fond memories of climbing that big beautiful tree and gorging on fresh avocados.

Many a hot summer evening we would chow down on fresh guacamole and chips. To this day I still love fresh guacamole! So much so that often on hot summer campouts it is not only an appetizer, but a dinner ~ a huge bowl of guacamole and chips. To me, guacamole is so easy, so refreshing, and the best food ever!

4 Servings

> 2 large avocados, seeded, peeled and coarsely mashed
>
> 2 tablespoons lime juice
>
> 2 cloves garlic, minced
>
> 2 small tomatoes, chopped
>
> ½ onion, chopped
>
> ⅔ chili pepper, minced
>
> 2 tablespoons cilantro (optional)
>
> 1 bag of tortilla chips

Mash the avocado and then blend with lemon juice, garlic, tomato, onion, chili pepper, and cilantro.

Set out the guacamole and a big bowl of tortilla chips, call for appetizers and watch it rapidly disappear! Everyone seems to love guacamole and chips.

Popcorn

Fresh popcorn as an appetizer, why had I not thought of that until 2013? That's when I found myself guiding on the Rio Maranon in Peru alongside Pedro, a Peruvian guide who serves popcorn all the time on the river and camp-outs.

Fresh popcorn is common in Peru, but many of us have lost the art of making it, so here you go an old-time USA tradition too ~ fresh popcorn. Great on the river!

Yields about 10 cups

> 2 to 4 tablespoons oil (for cooking the kernels)
>
> ½ cup popcorn kernels
>
> ¼ cup margarine
>
> Salt, to taste

It's best to cook popcorn in a large, heavy-bottomed pot. If you do not have a heavy bottomed pot you will need to watch it and shimmy the pot more in order to not burn the popped corn.

Over medium heat, combine the oil and 2 popcorn kernels. Be sure the inside bottom of the pot is completely covered with oil. Cover the pot and place on medium heat, wait for the kernels to pop. This might take a few minutes.

In the meantime, place a large serving bowl near the stove so it's ready when you need it.

Once the kernels pop, turn off the burner, remove the pot from the heat and pour in the remaining popcorn kernels. Cover the pot again, and give the pot a little shimmy to distribute the kernels evenly.

Let the pot rest for 60 seconds to make sure the oil doesn't get too hot before the kernels are ready to pop.

Turn the heat back up to medium, put the pot back onto the burner and continue cooking the popcorn, carefully shimmying the pot occasionally to cook the kernels evenly. Once the kernels start popping, tip the lid just a touch to allow steam to escape.

Continue cooking until the popping sound slows to about one pop every few seconds. If the popcorn tries to overflow the pot, just tip the upper portion of popcorn into your bowl and return it to the heat.

Remove the lid and dump the popcorn into your serving bowl.

Melt the margarine in another pan and pour over the popcorn. Add salt to taste. Toss and serve.

Soups ~ Instant

I often have soups as an appetizer because soup is a delicious and filling way to help ensure everyone is consuming water and staying hydrated.

Some people have a tendency to not drink enough water, resulting in headaches and other complications of dehydration.

With a tasty soup appetizer, you will have the added security of knowing you and your friends are consuming additional water, which is so essential to feeling your best and staying healthy while playing in the outdoors.

One of my favorites for Asian themed dinners is Sweet and Sour Instant Soup or Miso.

Knorr makes a lot of different varieties of instant soups that are very good. If you like creamy soups, here's a recipe for you.

Cream of Leek Soup

Serves 4

> 2 (1.8 ounce) packages Knorr Cream of Leek soup mix
>
> ¼ cup dry whole milk powder (NIDO)
>
> 5 cups water

First reconstitute the milk in the water, with whisk, stir until all lumps are gone. Add soup mix and follow the cooking directions on the packets.

PB2 Dipping Sauce with Veggies

PB2 is a versatile lightweight and pure dried peanut product.

4 Servings

Sauce

> 6 tablespoons PB2 powder
>
> 1 tablespoon soy sauce
>
> 3 tablespoons water
>
> ¼ teaspoon garlic powder
>
> ¼ teaspoon ground pepper
>
> ¼ teaspoon garlic chili sauce or ancho chili powder
>
> 2 teaspoons brown sugar
>
> ¼ teaspoon sesame oil or other vegetable oil

Vegetables

> 3 cups mixed vegetables, red bell peppers, jicama, carrots…

Cut up the vegetable into sticks: mix the PB2, soy sauce, water, oil, sugar and spices well; add more water a teaspoon at a time if you prefer a thinner dip.

Variation: place some of the vegetables into a Napa Cabbage leaf and turn it into a cabbage roll. Then dip in the peanut sauce.

Testimonials

Our absolute favorite recipe that we added to our repertoire during our sailing adventures has been the spring rolls out of your cookbook for no fridge no cooking. It is absolutely fantastic! We can't eat enough of them, and I have served them as appetizers to guests as well and they can't stop eating them either! It is a great recipe because the only fresh ingredients are things that last forever such as cabbage, carrots and onions... So when I want to make something special but haven't had access to a store, I just whip out this recipe and I am crowned wizard of the day. I tell everyone who asks, where I got the recipe. You are famous!
Cindy Patrinellis

Yummy and simple recipes. I ordered this book a few weeks ago and have gone through a good chunk of the recipes. All have been very good with many that worked for my vegan family members staying with us. I've packaged some of the recipes using freeze-dried ingredients for camping this fall and look forward to having such a simple and yummy menu.
Jamie Dalton

These are great! My son is celiac and a lot of the vegan meals are also gluten free. Love it.
Lynn Marie

A well-organized book, easy too. Yummy cooler-free camping! What a treat! Lacey introduced me to some new products and new ways to prepare. You can usually find me in the woods or on the water; and I like to eat well. In the past, eating well meant coolers, and heavy kitchen tools. This book keeps all the flavor and ritual of fine camp dining, but lightens the load and simplifies multi-day planning.
A keeper!
Julie T.

MAIN COURSE ~ DAYS 1 TO 6

Days 1 to 6: Fresh & Healthy – use the following recipes during the first 6 days of a long trip.

For the main course I recommend a multi-course dinner, starting with happy hour cocktails, beer or wine and appetizers.

The main course should be served with a side dish.

Round out the multi-course meal with a delicious dessert.

The special touch of serving a multi-course meal for dinner consisting of appetizer, main course, side dish and dessert results in people realizing that the meal plan has been well thought out. It lets participants know they are being well taken care of.

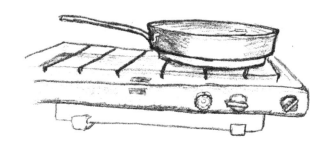

Red Coconut Curry

The vegetables and quantities are only a guideline, be creative and use your favorite vegetables and curry paste brand. You may want more curry paste for a stronger curry flavor or you may prefer a bit of sugar for sweetness. This is a recipe that really becomes your own, depending on your vegetable choices and your preferred brand of curry. I have left white space on the following page for you to jot down your notes for future reference.*

4 Servings

> 3 tablespoons olive oil
>
> 1 small onion
>
> 2 cloves garlic
>
> 3 carrots
>
> 1 small head of cauliflower
>
> 1 small sweet potato
>
> 1 small potato

Curry Sauce

> 2 tablespoons red curry paste
>
> 1 (13.5 ounce) can coconut milk
>
> 1 tablespoon brown sugar (optional)

Rice

> 2 cups rice
>
> 4 cups water
>
> 1 teaspoon salt
>
> 1 tablespoon oil

60

Toppings

>   1 small can water chestnuts, sliced

>   ½ cup raisins (optional)

>   ½ cup peanuts (optional)

Start the rice first because rice can take a long time to cook (unless you are using instant). Prepare everything else while the rice is cooking.

Chop all the vegetables, mince the garlic. Stir-fry the veggies in the oil. Cook veggies until they are almost done, firm and not mushy.

Make the curry sauce. Add the curry paste to the coconut milk and simmer for 5 minutes. Taste the curry sauce to determine if it needs more paste for a spicier flavor or add some brown sugar if it needs a little sweetness. Add the curry sauce to the vegetables and heat through.

To Serve: top the rice with the curried vegetables. Set out the water chestnuts, raisins and peanuts as additional toppings.

*Notes for Future Reference

_____

_____

_____

_____

_____

North African Couscous with Harissa

This recipe has lots of fresh ingredients, so it is best prepared on one of the first nights of your journey.

4 Servings

      ½ medium size onion, chopped

      ½ red bell pepper, seeded and chopped

      1 (7 ounce) can diced tomatoes (do not drain)

      1 ¼ cups grated carrots or 1 package (4 ounce) shredded carrots

      1 (15 ounce) can garbanzo beans, drained

      ¼ cup dried cranberries (craisins)

      ¼ cup raisins

      1 ½ tablespoons ground cumin

      1 tablespoon paprika

      ½ tablespoon ground cinnamon

      ¾ cup dry couscous

      ¾ cup water

      Pinch of salt

      ½ teaspoon margarine

      ½ cup chopped cashews or peanuts (optional)

Harissa (spicy condiment)

2 small cloves garlic, finely chopped

2 key limes, juiced

¼ teaspoon to 1 tablespoon red pepper flakes

3 tablespoons dehydrated tomato powder

Prepare the Harissa first: combine finely chopped garlic, pepper flakes, lime juice, and tomato powder in small bowl. Add water slowly, a tablespoon at a time, while mixing to desired consistency. It should be a thick sauce. Set aside. Note: you can substitute 1 can (6 ounce) of tomato paste for the tomato powder and water.

Prepare the Vegetables and Beans: Chop the fresh vegetables. Combine the onion, bell pepper and tomatoes (with juice) in a large saucepan. Bring to a boil; cover and simmer until onions are soft and translucent (about 10 minutes). Add the garbanzo beans, carrots, raisins, cranberries, cumin, paprika, and cinnamon to the vegetable mixture. Mix well and simmer for 5 minutes. You may need to add water to prevent sticking.

Couscous: as the vegetables simmer prepare the dry couscous. Bring the water, salt, and margarine to a boil. Add couscous, stirring quickly. Remove from heat and cover. Let stand for 4 to 5 minutes.

To Serve: fluff couscous with a fork and add to vegetable mixture. Mix well. Top individual servings with Harissa and optional cashews or peanuts.

Chop Suey de Peru

Let the local in-season produce from organic markets determine the produce to use. Come up with your own favorite combination of vegetables to personalize this recipe. I like the produce listed in the recipe because it is normally easy to find and common, but you may have other favorites. I have left white space on the following page for you to jot down your notes for future reference.*

4 Servings

> ½ cabbage, sliced thin -1/8-inch thick
>
> 2 carrots, sliced thin
>
> 1 red onion
>
> 1 bell pepper, small
>
> 4 cloves garlic
>
> 1 (thumb-sized) piece of fresh ginger
>
> ¼ cup soy sauce
>
> 1 cube vegetable stock (bullion)
>
> 2 tablespoons oil or more for frying
>
> 1 cup dry roasted peanuts (optional)

Rice

> 2 cups rice
>
> 4 cups water
>
> 1 teaspoon salt
>
> 1 tablespoon oil

Rice can take a long time to cook (unless you use instant); you should prepare everything else while the rice is cooking. Follow the directions on the package or my recipe for Basic Rice.

Slice the cabbage very thin. Cook the cabbage and carrots in large pot for about 15 minutes, cabbage should be still somewhat crisp, but done.

Peel and slice the ginger very thinly. Chop the remaining vegetables. In a large fry pan, sauté the onions and peppers for a few minutes in a tablespoon or so of oil. Add the ginger and garlic, adding more oil if needed. Sauté a few minutes and add the bouillon cube and soy sauce, stir and remove from flame.

Once the cabbage and carrots are done, drain as much water as possible from cabbage and add to the fried onions, peppers, ginger and garlic.

Serve the vegetables chop suey over rice, top with peanuts.

*Notes for Future Reference

_____

_____

_____

_____

_____

_____

_____

Hearty Lentil Vegetarian Stew

Lentils are a staple of mine; red lentils cook the fastest. Red lentils in reality come in a variety of colors, ranging from gold, to orange and to red.

There are many varieties of lentils, but the basic five are brown, green, red, black and yellow. In general, the brown and green varieties retain their shape well, whereas red tend to disintegrate and thicken dishes, therefore, red are best for soup and can be used as a thickening agent.

4 Servings

> 1 tablespoon olive oil
>
> 1 onion, chopped
>
> 4 cloves garlic, minced
>
> 2 carrots, sliced
>
> 4 ¼ cups water
>
> 2 cubes vegetable bouillon
>
> 1 ½ cups lentils, rinsed and picked through
>
> 1 or 2 large potatoes, peeled and cut into large chunks
>
> 1 teaspoon dried oregano
>
> ½ teaspoon dried cumin
>
> ¼ teaspoon cayenne pepper
>
> 1 teaspoon salt
>
> ½ teaspoon black pepper
>
> 2 limes, quartered

In a large saucepan over medium heat, warm the olive oil. Add the onions, garlic, and carrots. Cover and cook until the onions have softened, stirring often, for about 10 minutes.

Add the water, vegetable stock, lentils, potato chunks, oregano, cumin, cayenne, salt and pepper. Turn the heat to high and bring to a boil. Reduce heat to low, cover and simmer for about 35 or 45 more minutes, or until lentils and potatoes are fully cooked. Add more water if needed.

Serve with quartered limes on the side for squeezing juice onto stew.

Falafel

Many times, I have made falafels at home but had never thought of making them on the river until guiding a week-long river trip on the Rio Usumacinta in Chiapas, Mexico. A fellow guide included falafels on the menu, hence I discovered just how easy it is to serve from the camp kitchen as well.

I have included two sauces in this recipe, one is a cucumber sauce which I enjoy for the freshness it adds to the robust flavors of this dish and then a recipe for the traditional Tahini sauce. Please see the sauce recipes following this recipe for preparation directions for both sauces.

4 Servings

> 2 cups falafel mix*, (2 [8 ounce] boxes of Fantastic World Food Falafel Mix)
>
> 2 ¼ cups water
>
> 2 tomatoes, sliced
>
> 1 or 2 scallions, thin sliced
>
> 4 lemons, (2 quartered and 2 more to juice for tahini recipe)
>
> ½ small head Napa cabbage, very thin sliced
>
> ¾ cup cooking oil (possible a bit more)
>
> 4 Pita Pockets (burrito-size flour tortillas can be substituted if you prefer)

Mix the water with the falafel mix (follow the directions and water quantity on the package). Let the mix stand for 15 minutes to absorb the water.

While the falafel mix rehydrates (about 15 minutes), prepare the veggies and sauces. Slice the tomatoes, thinly slice the onions and very thinly slice the cabbage (shred) and then prepare the sauces.

Falafel: form into round balls about 1 to 2 inches in diameter. If the texture is too dry to form balls, add 1 teaspoon of water at a time until desired consistency is reached. Flatten the balls into ½" thick patties. Heat the oil on a medium flame in a tall sided frying pan.

Carefully drop the patties into the hot oil. You will want the oil to be hot enough to quickly brown the outside, thereby making the patties easier to flip and cook correctly. Cook for 3 to 4 minutes on 1 side and then very carefully flip and cook another 3 to 4 minutes, until brown and crispy. Remove patties from the oil and set on paper towels to absorb excess oil.

Make both the Tahini and the Cucumber sauce now, following directions on following page.

To Serve: cut pita pockets in half, fill with a few falafel patties, squeeze lemon juice over patties, add tomatoes, scallions and cabbage, top with sauces. If there is additional sauce and veggies, serve those on the side.

Variation: serve with large flour tortillas, Flatbread or Naan in place of the Pita Pockets.

*Falafel mix is made from dried Garbanzo beans, aka Chickpeas. Garbanzo beans are an excellent choice for vegetarians and vegans as they are rich in protein.

Tahini and Cucumber Sauces

Tahini is the traditional middle-eastern sauce for falafels. The sesame seed-based tahini adds even more nutrition to this recipe, fabulous for the vegetarians and vegans on your trip.

I enjoy cucumber sauce for the freshness it adds to the robust flavors of the falafel.

4 Servings

Cucumber Sauce

> 1 small English cucumber, sliced
>
> 2 cups shelf stable Greek Yogurt Dressing or Ranch Dressing

Tahini Sauce

> 2 lemons, juiced
>
> 2 cloves garlic, minced
>
> ⅔ cup Tahini
>
> Pinch of sugar

Cucumber Sauce: thinly slice then coarsely chop some of the cucumber, leave part of the cucumber in slices in order to serve cucumber slices on the side. Mix the coarsely chopped cucumbers with the ranch dressing, set aside.

Tahini Sauce: combine the juice from 2 lemons, the garlic, and start blending in the tahini a little bit at a time. Mix completely, wait a minute to determine the consistency of the paste. Add water to your desired consistency. Use a pinch of sugar and salt to taste.

Tasty Bites with Rice

Serve a variety of Tasty Bites so people can mix and match. I like to add fresh potatoes because it bulks up the Tasty Bites a bit. Sweet potatoes or yams are also a good addition. Using instant rice insures this super easy dinner stays that way – super easy and fast!

4 Servings

> 2 cups instant white rice (Minute Brand)
>
> 2 cups water
>
> 3 Tasty Bites packets, varieties of your choice*
>
> 2 potatoes, peeled and diced (optional)

If you are using fresh potatoes. Peel, dice, and cook them first, drain and set-aside when done.

Prepare the instant rice. Bring 2 cups of water to a boil. Stir in 2 cups of rice and cover. Remove from heat. Let stand for 5 minutes or until water is absorbed. As the rice is cooking heat up the Tasty Bites packets in a pot of boiling water.

If you are using the fresh potatoes, as the rice cooks, open the Tasty Bite packets and pour in some of the drained potatoes and heat till hot.

To serve: place rice in bowl or plate and top with Tasty Bite mixture.

*Tasty Bites are instant, pre-packaged meal topper for rice. All of the varieties are inspired by Indian food. They come in handy pouches and are healthy and flavorful.

SIDE DISHES ~ DAYS 1 TO 6

Days 1 to 6: Fresh & Healthy – use the following recipes during the first 6 days of a long trip.

Basic Rice

I often use instant rice in the Camp Without Coolers kitchen because it is so quick and easy, but everyone should know how to make homemade rice when there is plenty of time to cook. Just in case you are not sure how to make homemade rice I have included this basic rice recipe.

4 Servings

> 4 cups water
>
> 2 cups rice
>
> 1 teaspoon salt
>
> 1 tablespoon oil or margarine

Add salt to water and bring to a boil in a covered saucepan. Add rice and coconut oil and return to boiling. Cover and reduce heat to lowest flame. Simmer for 20 minutes, check to see if done. If not done cook for 10 minutes more. Let sit for 5 minutes, fluff and serve.

Tip: when cooking rice, put a spoon into the pot, gently push the rice aside, and check the bottom to see if the water has been absorbed; do not over stir, as it will become starchy.

Colorful Carrot Slaw

This recipe holds many good memories for me. Everytime I make this, I am transported back to the Rio Usumacinta in Mexico. I was hired as a camp chef and captain for one of the gear boats. I remember grating carrots while gazing out over the river and at an archological wonder left by the Mayan Civilization. The Mayans had carved a symbol into a giant riverside rock. Archeologis believe it was a sign for the entrance into their deep jungle city of Piedras Negras.

As I grated carrots my mind wondered to what that symbol meant? Was it a welcome or a warning? I hope that when you prepare this recipe you too are having an amazing time and can gaze in wonder at your surroundings.

This recipe is a bit of work, but well worth the effort to have fresh carrot slaw. For me, it is actually relaxing to hand-grate 4 carrots while preparing a healthful salad for all.

3 to 4 Servings

> 4 carrots, grated
>
> 2 oranges
>
> 2 tablespoons sunflower seeds
>
> 2 tablespoons pumpkin seeds
>
> 1 tablespoon sesame seeds
>
> 1 tablespoon chia seeds
>
> 2 teaspoons agave nectar

Peel and section the orange. Squeeze about ¼ of the orange (juice) over the grated carrots. Slice up the rest of the orange and add to carrots. Add the seeds and agave nectar, mix well and serve.

Homemade Garlic Naan

This recipe yields a very soft, chewy, garlicky naan - yum!

This is one of the more challenging recipes to make in the camp kitchen, but I believe it is worth the effort. I placed this recipe in this first section of the cookbook because it goes really nicely with many dishes, you may decide to serve it later in the trip as well. Play around with this recipe before your journey to help you decide which week to prepare.

Tip for preparing this recipe later in an extended length expedition: replace the stick margarine with shortening. While I do not recommend eating shortening on a regular bases, I do believe it is fine in small quantities, on occasion. Shortening keeps really well without ice or refrigeration. I use it, but only sporadically and only while doing extended camping trips or making that perfect pie crust at home.

Many people will appreciate fresh bread, especially on long expeditions, such as a Grand Canyon river trip. By the third week fresh breads are often stale and people are tiring of crackers. Add this to your recipe collection as back-up.

Yields 8 pieces of naan

> 1 ½ cups warm water
>
> 1 tablespoon sugar
>
> 2 teaspoons active dry yeast
>
> 1 teaspoon salt
>
> 3 cups white flour, plus a few tablespoons for dusting flour onto the workspace
>
> 6 cloves garlic
>
> 6 tablespoons stick margarine

Combine warm water, sugar, and yeast in a bowl. Let stand for 5 minutes until foamy.

Add salt and flour to the yeast water. Mix thoroughly. Knead dough on a floured workspace about 20 times and form into a tight ball. Put dough in a well-oiled bowl and cover with a damp towel. Put in a warm place to rise for 30-45 minutes. The dough won't rise much, but it doesn't need to.

Mince garlic and sauté in margarine for a few minutes. Turn dough onto a floured workspace. Divide dough into 8 pieces. If I were to make this at home, I would use a rolling pin, but while camping one can improvise. A Nalgene bottle will work in place of a rolling pin. Wash and completely dry the bottle. Using the bottle as a rolling pin flatten dough to about 1/8" thick (like a tortilla).

Place a little bit of margarine in a frying pan. Spray oil is not necessary, but if you have some spray oil, that works well. In the fry pan, cook each naan over a medium high flame for 2 minutes or so on each side. If you do not have a timer then cook until bubbles form and is slightly browned one each side. Note: you want the pan to be hot enough that the bread forms bubbles pretty quickly as they cook, but not so hot that it burns.

As each piece of bread finishes cooking, brush naan with a bit of the garlic margarine and stack on plate until all are cooked. When all are done serve the plate of naan to your guests alongside the main course.

Crunchy Salt Cured Tofu

The keys to delicious tofu are (1) buy good tofu, (2) get the tofu as dry as possible before frying, (3) fry in a hot skillet with a decent amount of oil, (4) don't crowd the pan, and (5) cook until it is really brown.

> 1 (12 ounce) box, extra firm tofu in shelf stable UHT box*
>
> 2 tablespoons salt
>
> 2 cups water
>
> 2 to 4 tablespoons oil
>
> 2 unused clean dishtowels or many paper towels
>
> 2 large firm cutting boards or 1 large cutting board and a firm clean table top

Carefully open the tofu package so as not to crumble the tofu. Drain the water, and cut tofu into slabs a little over ¼" thick. Carefully lay the slabs into pan for soaking. The salt-cured tofu will give a nice ratio of crust to interior during frying.

First, add salt to water and bring to a boil and pour it over the tofu slices to completely cover. Let this stand for about 15 minutes, then prepare to press the tofu.

The second step (pressing) is what is going to help the tofu to brown nicely when fried. Very carefully pick up the delicate slabs of tofu and lay them in a single layer on clean cutting board, covered with a dishtowel (or towel covered clean tabletop). Put another clean dishtowel on top of the tofu slices. Fold the length of paper towels or a dishcloth in half or quarters to increase the absorbency. Place a cutting board on top of

76

the cloth covered tofu slices and place a weight on top of the cutting board.

Your weight should be heavy enough to press down evenly across the top of the tofu, but not so heavy so as to cause the tofu block to crumble. A large can of food will work as a weight. Other objects that might work include an iron frying pan, a heavy book, etc. Let the tofu sit for at least 30 minutes. The weight will gradually and effectively squeeze out the moisture in the tofu, where it will be absorbed by the dishcloth/paper towels. If the paper towels become fully saturated, you may need to replace them with fresh paper towels and continue pressing until the paper towels stop absorbing moisture.

After 30 minutes (or when there is no more or very little moisture left in tofu), proceed with cooking the tofu.

Heat a skillet over high to medium high heat. Once hot, add about 2 tablespoons of oil. Use oil with a high smoke point (vegetable, canola or peanut are good choices). Cover the bottom of the pan with a thin layer of oil, but not enough to cause a lot of hot oil popping out of the pan. Start with about 2 tablespoons and add more if needed.

Pat the tofu dry one more time and very carefully place the tofu in the skillet in a single layer, with plenty of room around each piece. You may want to try one piece as a sizzle test to make sure the oil is hot enough. Once this piece begins to sizzle, add more slabs. Cover pan with a splash screen because oil may be popping up. Don't crowd the pan, or the heat will drop too much and the tofu will steam, not brown. Cook on one side until it is a **deep golden brown**, then flip (about 2 to 3 minutes) and brown the other side. It is impractical to brown the edges of each piece, so instead just brown the large, flat sides of the slab. When both sides are done, place tofu on paper towels to absorb excess oil and set aside.

If you are going to turn the tofu into a stir-fry, don't be tempted to add the vegetables and sauce on top of the tofu. It will ruin the crust. Instead, remove the tofu from the pan, fry your vegetables, then add the tofu back just in time for it to make friends with the sauce.

*Tofu in a shelf-stable UHT box. The UHT acronym simply stands for aseptic packaging of tofu using Ultra High Temperature (UHT). The soy bean milk is processed prior to packaging with the use of high temperatures (135–150°C) for short periods of time (a few seconds) to achieve a product that is commercially sterile.

The UHT process allows for boxed tofu to be stored on the shelf (no refrigeration needed) and for much longer periods of time without refrigeration.

Choose an extra-firm tofu with an expiration date well into the future. The date is often a better indicator of quality than the brand. That being said, I have been very happy with the Mori-Nu brand.

Tofu is an excellent source of protein for vegetarians and vegans. Consider adding it to your diet because tofu is high in protein, a good source of calcium, is cholesterol free and low in saturated fat protein.

Creamy Cabbage Slaw

This recipe was handed down to me by my dear friend and outdoor mentor Bob Marley, only his recipe utilized dried cabbage and this recipe uses fresh cabbage.

4 Servings

> 1 apple
>
> ½ cabbage (Napa* or green)
>
> 10 tablespoons mayonnaise (vegan mayonnaise)
>
> 1 tablespoon sugar
>
> ½ cup cider vinegar

Peel, core and dice the apple. Slice the cabbage into thin slivers, add to the diced apple and top with sugar, and vinegar. Mix in mayonnaise (note: the recipe calls for 10 tablespoons but this is an individual taste sort of thing – add 1 tablespoon at a time until it is to your liking). Add salt and pepper to taste.

*Napa Cabbage is my favorite because it has a more delicate texture and milder flavor than green or red cabbage, making it perfect for eating raw. It has a distinctive barrel-shape with a thick white rib and crisp, pale green, tightly-wrapped leaves. It will stay fresh for a few weeks without a cooler if cared for properly; kept out of the sun and extreme heat. Best to leave the heads whole and don't wash or cut them until you're ready to prep.

Asian Quinoa

A versatile dish because you can make a heartier version by adding tofu, eggs (protein of your choice) and more vegetables. Pack it with all that additional good stuff to take it from a basic side dish to a full-on dinner.

This recipe goes well with the creamy cabbage slaw.

4 Servings

> 2 tablespoons olive oil
>
> 1 cup Quinoa
>
> 2 cups water
>
> 1 cube vegetable bouillon
>
> 2 tablespoons soy sauce
>
> 1 clove garlic, finely chopped or grated
>
> 1 tablespoon ginger, finely chopped or grated
>
> 1 teaspoon Thai chili paste/sauce (optional)

Read the label on the quinoa, is it prewashed? If not, do rinse first before preparing meal. A cheesecloth works nicely for rinsing the small grains of quinoa.

Heat olive oil in medium saucepan. Add quinoa and toast for about 2 minutes, stirring frequently. Add broth, soy sauce, garlic, ginger, and chili sauce; bring to a boil. Cover and simmer on low heat until broth is absorbed, about 20 minutes. Fluff with a fork and serve.

Super-Fast Lentils

This recipe is so easy and tasty it is my go-to recipe when I want a chill night as the camp chef. I make it on almost every long river expedition, saving it for the last day when I want a lighter kitchen duty day. Quick, tasty, easy!

4 Servings

> 1 small onion or 1 medium shallot, chopped
>
> 1 clove garlic, minced
>
> 1 carrot, chopped
>
> 1 (15 ounce) can lentils, drained
>
> 1 (7 ounce) can black beans, drained
>
> 1 tablespoon oil

Chop the veggies, mince garlic and sauté the veggie mix in oil. Drain the lentils and beans and add to the sautéed vegetables.

Heat thoroughly, add spices of your choice, and serve.

Lentils are considered a superfood. Especially good for vegetarians and vegans. Ounce for ounce, lentils have as much protein as steak (with less than 10 percent of the fat). And as noted in many nutritional studies, a diet high in lentils and other legumes can reduce your risk of cancer, diabetes and heart disease.

DESSERTS ~ DAYS 1 TO 6

Days 1 to 6: Fresh & Healthy – use the following recipes during the first 6 days of a long trip.

No-Bake Peanut Butter Chocolate Bars

Everyone loves a delicious No-Bake, No-Fuss dessert, especially the camp cook!

Yields 16 (2×2 inch) bars

>   1 cup peanut butter, chunky
>
>   ¾ cup honey
>
>   3 cups quick (instant) oatmeal
>
>   ½ cup craisins
>
>   1 cup Nutella

Combine the peanut butter and honey in a medium saucepan and warm over low heat, stirring constantly until mixed thoroughly. Remove from heat and add in the oatmeal and craisins. Press into a 9×9-inch ungreased pan and let cool.

Place in a Bucket Refrigerator (see following page) to speed up cooling process.

Spread the Nutella on top of cooled oat mixture. Cut into bars and set out on serving plate.

Bucket Refrigerator: use this technique in place of a cooler for chilling desserts. Requires a 1-gallon zip lock freezer bag and 1 extra-large bucket (like the NRS "Big Basin Water Container").

Step 1

Carefully place the dessert in a 1-gallon Zip-Lock Freezer Bag and seal completely. Be sure no water can leak in through the top of the bag.

Step 2

Fill the bucket with cool water. Float the dessert (which has been placed inside a zip lock baggie) in cool water (creek or river). Double check that the zip lock is securely closed so that no water can get into bag and ruin the pie. Be extra careful that the top of the bag is not lying in the water.

Key Lime Dessert de Veracruz

I learned the basics of making this traditional Mexican dessert while attending a Spanish school in Veracruz, Mexico. This is one of my most requested dessert recipes.

Yields 1 pie

>   ¾ cup lime juice, fresh squeezed (about 4 big, juicy limes)
>
>   1 can evaporated milk
>
>   1 can sweetened condensed milk
>
>   2 tablespoons Ultra Gel
>
>   1 package Maria´s Cookies

Squeeze the fresh limes for juice.

Blend the milks together. Blend in the lime juice. The acid in the lime juice may cause the milk to "curdle," don't be alarmed. Add the Ultra Gel and whisk to a creamy consistency. It will start to thicken fairly quickly, so act fast for the next step.

Place one layer of cookies on the bottom of pie tin and around the edges forming a "crust." Pour in half of the pie mixture, then another layer of cookies. Pour in the remaining pie mixture and level the surface with a spatula.

Place in a Bucket Refrigerator (see directions for the Bucket Refrigerator on the prior page).

Please note: even if you do not have a way to chill this dessert it will still set-up and thicken, it will just take a bit longer without a cooling system.

84

Homemade Fudge with Strawberries

At dinner time, it is wisest to make the fudge at the same time as the appetizer because that will give it the time needed to cool. Top with any kind of fresh berries for a flavor delight!

Yields 1 pound

¼ cup stick margarine

1 cup sugar

¼ cup evaporated milk

⅔ cup semi-sweet chocolate chips

½ cup marshmallow cream

⅛ teaspoon vanilla

¼ cup walnuts, chopped

15 fresh strawberries

Combine stick margarine, sugar and milk in heavy large saucepan. Over low heat, bring to a complete full boil, stirring constantly. Add remaining ingredients. Stir vigorously, making sure the chocolate chips and marshmallow cream are dissolved.

Continue boiling for 5 minutes, stirring constantly to avoid scorching. Remove from heat.

Pour into a greased pan. Let completely cool. You can use a Bucket Refrigerator to speed cooling.

To Serve: cut the leaves and stems from the fresh strawberries. Cut fudge into 1-inch squares. Top each fudge square with a fresh strawberry.

Raspberry No-Bake Cheesecake

You may have had a no-bake cheesecake at some point, but I bet you never had one with this delicious homemade Raspberry Glaze topping with a Chocolate Drizzle – Yum!

Yields 1 pie

> 1 box Cheesecake Mix
>
> 1 ½ cups milk (boxed, whole milk)
>
> 6 tablespoons coconut oil
>
> 2 tablespoons sugar (white)
>
> 2 tablespoons Ultra Gel

Raspberry Glaze (makes about 2 cups)

> 1 ½ cups (1.5 ounce) freeze-dried raspberries
>
> 1 ½ cups water
>
> ½ cup sugar
>
> 1 tablespoon lemon juice
>
> ¼ cup of Ultra Gel

Make the Topping First: place freeze-dried raspberries, water, sugar, and lemon juice in a pan. Bring to a boil and set aside to cool. Cool for at least ½ hour. After it is cooled, slowly add Ultra Gel and stir thoroughly with a wire whisk to remove any lumps.

Pie Crust: stir crust mix from boxed cheesecake, 2 tablespoons sugar, 6 tablespoons coconut oil and 1 tablespoon water thoroughly in a mixing bowl until crumbs are well moistened. Place in a pie tin and firmly press crumbs to coat the inside of the tin.

Pie Filling: pour 1 ½ cups milk into bowl. Add filling mix from boxed cheesecake. Beat until blended. Add Ultra Gel; beat until blended. Beat for three more minutes. The filling should be thick. Spoon into the crust. Chill until the filling is set. My Bucket Refrigerator cooling system works well (see Bucket Refrigerator page).

Once the cheesecake is firm, pour the Raspberry Glaze on top, slice and serve.

Chocolate Drizzle

This chocolate drizzle can be used for many different types of dessert, including the Rum Balls and many more recipes!

> 2 tablespoons unsweetened cocoa
>
> 1 cup powdered sugar
>
> 2 tablespoons coconut oil or shortening
>
> 2 tablespoons hot water
>
> ½ teaspoon vanilla extract
>
> ¼ teaspoon salt

Stir together cocoa powder, powdered sugar and salt in a bowl. Combine hot water, shortening and vanilla in another bowl. Pour this liquid into dry cocoa mixture, mixing until smooth.

Drizzle over dessert. It will harden as it cools

No-Bake Coconut Chocolate Cookies

Everyone loves a delicious No-Bake, No-Fuss to prepare dessert, especially if it's chocolate!

This dessert is great for an evening that you want to prepare a fresh dessert, but not spend much additional time in the camp kitchen. All that is required is having the ingredients on-hand, doing a little boiling over the camp stove, mixing the ingredients and waiting for the cookies to set.

Yields 12 cookies

>   1 cup quick cooking oats
>
>   ½ cup shredded coconut
>
>   2 tablespoons cocoa powder
>
>   1 cup sugar
>
>   ¼ cup coconut oil
>
>   ¾ tablespoon milk powder
>
>   ¼ cup water

Mix oats, coconut and cocoa powder together in a bowl.

Reconstitute the milk powder in the ¼ cup of water. Pour in a saucepan and add the sugar and coconut oil; bring the milk mixture to a full rolling boil, stirring constantly. Boil for 5 seconds, remove immediately from heat and stir into oat mixture.

Drop batter by the spoonful (about 12) onto a sheet of waxed or parchment paper. Cool to room temperature before serving. The longer the cookies sit the firmer they become.

~~~~~~~~~~~~~~~~~~~~~~~~~~~~~~~~~~~~

WEEK 2
DAYS 7 TO 12

~ QUICK & EASY ~

It is important to use the following recipes during the
second week of a long trip.

The ingredients in the recipes for days 7 through 12
will last into the second week of an 18-day journey,
but need to be eaten during the second week because
they have a limited shelf life consisting of semi-
perishable fresh items, canned goods and dried items.

Kick the Cooler Habit!

~~~~~~~~~~~~~~~~~~~~~~~~~~~~~~~~~~~~

BREAKFAST ~ DAYS 7 TO 12

Breakfast Buffet

I often make meals that are served buffet style because people can pick and choose which items and the quantity of items that they prefer.

4 Servings

> ½ pound granola (2 cups) or cereal of choice
>
> 1 cup nuts of choice
>
> 1 cup dried fruits (raisins, craisins, dates, figs)
>
> 2 tablespoons chia seeds
>
> ¼ cup Cacao Nibs or pure Cacao beans
>
> ¾ quart soy or nut milk, boxed
>
> ½ quart soy yogurt, optional
>
> 4 apples or oranges
>
> 1 (16 ounce) can peaches
>
> 8 breakfast or energy bars

Open the can of peaches and set everything out buffet style. Guests can top their cereal with items of their choice.

Each person takes a piece of fruit and energy bar. If they do not eat it for breakfast, they can have it for a snack later.

Marley's Apple Pancakes

This recipe was inspired by Bob and Susan Marley. They led backpacking and river running adventures all over the world, specializing in the United States Southwest. Their group meals were most often on the lighter side, extremely creative, and always delicious!

I did my first Grand Canyon River trip in 1997 with this dynamic duo as the trip leaders. I was impressed with their simple camp kitchen set-up and meals. They were my first inspiration for something more appetizing than the basic PBJ sandwich while going light on an outdoor adventure

I became hooked on the idea of no coolers and started to experiment with recipes for my emerging camp without coolers philosophy due to Bob and Susan ~ thanks so much!

4 Servings

> 1 (8 ounce) can applesauce
>
> ¼ teaspoon cinnamon
>
> 3 cups pancake mix
>
> 1 (8 ounce) bottle maple syrup
>
> ½ cup stick margarine

Mix pancakes per directions on the box using applesauce in place of the water.

Place a dollop of margarine in fry pan or griddle and heat. Pour pancake mixture onto pan, making the cakes, cook until bubbles form, flip, and cook till they are a golden brown.

Serve with maple syrup and leftover applesauce if available.

Vegetarian Breakfast Burrito

Not just for the camp kitchen, this recipe is good at home too!

4 Hearty Servings

> 2 potatoes, cut into small cubes
>
> 1 onion, small or several green onions, chopped
>
> 1 small red bell pepper, chopped
>
> ⅓ cup oil
>
> ½ teaspoon garlic powder
>
> ½ teaspoon salt
>
> ½ teaspoon black pepper
>
> 1 (15 ounce) can pinto beans
>
> Flour Tortillas, large burrito size
>
> Salsa
>
> 4 to 6 eggs, (optional)
>
> 1 cup cheese, grated (optional)

Chop potatoes, onions, and fresh peppers. Add oil to a large fry pan. Heat the oil until hot. Add potatoes. Cook potatoes until just starting to be tender. Add onions and bell pepper. Fry 5 minutes more or so. Turn up the flame and cook under high heat until well browned.

If using eggs, add eggs to the potato mixture. Stir in the drained pinto beans. Cook a few minutes until eggs are done and beans are warm.

Place mixture onto tortillas, add salsa and optional cheese. Roll like a burrito.

Date Couscous

Inspiration again from my friends, the Marley's. Bob was one of the first to backpack the length of the Grand Canyon, thus he knows a thing or two about packing food for extended trips without coolers or ice.

4 Servings

⅔ cup dates or any other dried fruit

2 tablespoons stick margarine

1 ⅔ cups water for couscous

1 ¼ cups couscous

⅓ teaspoon salt

1 tablespoon sugar

¼ cup sunflower seeds, hulled and salted

⅓ to ½ cup dry whole milk powder (NIDO)

1 ½ cups water for milk

4 Breakfast Bars, Fruit filled

Dice the dates into fine pieces. Bring the water for the couscous and margarine to a boil. Add couscous, salt, sugar and dates, stirring constantly. Remove from heat, cover and let stand for 5 minutes.

Mix dry whole milk powder and water in a separate container to serve with couscous. Add more powder if you would like it creamier.

After couscous has sat for 5 minutes, stir well to distribute fruit evenly and fluff.

Serve breakfast with milk and breakfast bars.

Guatemalan Mosh

I learned the technique of preparing Mosh (an ancient Mayan hearty beverage) from indigenous Q'eqchi Maya whom I lived with for a couple months in the northern highlands of Guatemala. This delicious thick drink filled my tummy and warmed my soul on those cool mountain mornings.

It is traditional to serve Mosh with platanos (plantains). The plantains take longer to cook than the Mosh, so cook the plantains first. It is your choice for preparation technique, boiled or fried. My western palate really likes fried in butter, but it is simpler and more in line with tradition to serve boiled platanos (recipe on following page).

4 Servings

> 1 cup instant oatmeal
>
> 6 ½ cups water
>
> ½ teaspoon cinnamon
>
> 1 tablespoon sugar
>
> Sugar or other sweetener to taste

Place oatmeal, water, and cinnamon in a large pot. Bring to a boil, turn flame down and simmer for 5 minutes. Stir as needed to keep from scorching. Add more water as needed to maintain the consistency. Mosh is a thick drink not a porridge.

Serve the Mosh in large mugs with sugar or other sweeteners. Place the boiled or fried platanos on a plate as an accompaniment to the Mosh.

Eliza's Platanos

Eliza was a gracious host while I lived in the lowland region of northern Guatemala. I was studying Spanish and her family home was my home-away-from-home. She taught me a bit of Spanish and the cooking techniques for many traditional meals. Eliza's family often drank the hearty oat-based beverage called Mosh; she served Mosh alongside boiled platanos. She taught me the following preparation techniques for platanos.

4 Servings

> 2 plantains (platanos)
>
> Oil (if you fry the plantain)

In northern Guatemala, boiled plantain (platanos) and Mosh are the traditional morning meal. You can also fry plantains.

The plantain takes longer to cook than the Mosh, so cook the plantain first. It is your choice, boiled or fried.

Boiled Platanos: leave the skin on the plantain and cut it into 1" to 2" inch long pieces. Boil with the skin still intact for a half an hour or more. Remove skins after boiling to eat with the Mosh.

Fried Platanos: peel and slice the plantain into ½" thick pieces. Fry on a medium to high flame. Fry in oil on both sides until soft on the inside and crispy on the outside. This will take about 10 minutes.

Serve platanos with a big mug of Mosh. Great on the cool mornings!

LUNCH~ DAYS 7 TO 12

Days 7 to 12: Quick & Easy – use the following recipes during the second week of a long trip.

Tahini Spread

The fresh lemons are essential to this recipe. The juice from the fresh lemons causes the tahini to transform from a liquid into a spreadable paste.

Yields over 1 ½ cups, depending on how much lemon juice and water added.

> 2 lemons, juiced
>
> 2 cloves garlic, minced
>
> ⅔ cup Tahini (Mighty Sesame Co. Fine Sesame Tahini)
>
> Pinch of sugar
>
> Pinch of salt
>
> 1 (9 ounce) box Wheat Thins crackers

Combine lemon juice from 2 lemons and garlic.

Start blending in the tahini a little bit at a time.

Mix completely, wait a couple of minutes to determine the consistency of the paste. Add water to your desired consistency.

Add a pinch of sugar and/or salt to taste.

Use this recipe as a dip for crackers.

My favorite flavor combination is Wheat Thins crackers and this tahini spread.

Quick Trail Lunch

Great for a busy day.

This is my go-to lunch for a day when hiking is planned, or when people want to keep being active (hiking, boating, climbing, etc.) through lunchtime or when your group simply does not want to stop and take the time to set-up tables and such for a traditional group picnic.

I often set-out the Quick Trail Lunch items buffet style to be individually packaged and chosen from right after breakfast.

First hand out the individual containers and then people fill the container with the laid-out items listed below. Once done selecting, secure this individual lunch packages. They can then be eaten at the time that the individual decides is best. Be it while they are boating, hiking, or whenever they prefer to eat lunch throughout the day.

4 Servings

> 8 (1.15 ounce) nut butter spread packets (I prefer Justin's Nut Butter)
>
> 1 (13 ounce) box of crackers (your choice)
>
> 1 pound GORP, (see recipe following page)
>
> 8 apples
>
> 8 energy bars
>
> 1 (10 ounce) package cookies (optional)
>
> 4 baggies or containers for each person

Hand out individual baggies or containers so that each guest can assemble their own lunch as they choose.

Lay all out on a table and guests can grab the items to add to their individual baggie/containers.

Tomato Hummus Lime Wraps

Hummus means chickpea in Arabic. Hummus is a traditional Middle Eastern food made from dried garbanzo beans (chickpeas).

Hummus is also a popular USA dip and spread that is packed with vitamins and minerals. Research has linked hummus and its ingredients to a variety of health benefits, including helping to fight inflammation, improving blood sugar control, better digestive health, lower heart disease risk and weight loss.

Dried powdered hummus is an amazing non-perishable food item for the vegetarian following a no coolers philosophy. It is easy to prepare, tasty, high in protein and keeps a very long time without coolers, ice or refrigeration.

Yields approximately 2 cups

Hummus

> 1 cup dried hummus*
>
> 1 ½ cups water
>
> 3 tablespoons olive oil
>
> 1 lime, juiced
>
> ¼ teaspoon salt
>
> 1 cup sundried tomatoes, sliced (about 3-ounce package)

Serve with:

> 1 small head of Napa cabbage
>
> 4 Flatout bread pieces or some other Middle Eastern style of bread*

1 red pepper

1 carrot

½ red onion

1 jicama, small

1 English cucumber

Mix dried hummus, water, oil, juice of 1 lime, salt and ½ cup sundried tomatoes in a bowl. Set aside for approximately 5 minutes.

Slice the red pepper, carrot onion, jicama, and cucumber into thin slivers.

Assemble Wraps: first grab a piece of wrap/bread and lay a piece of cabbage on top of the bread. Place a couple tablespoons of hummus on the cabbage leaf, then place a few pieces of onion, bell pepper and carrot inside. Roll or fold to eat with your bare hands – Yum!

*Hummus Powder (Dried) is so handy; I keep powdered hummus in my home cupboards as well. It is easy to mix a batch up whenever I like. The powdered variety is just as tasty as fresh! There are no worries with storing it for long periods of time in the dried state. It can be found in most supermarkets and health food stores. Fantastic Foods is my preferred brand.

*Flatout Flatbread, Greek, Pita Pockets, Naan, burrito sized Flour Tortilla or whatever is your favorite wrap.

Ginger Soba Noodle Salad

To make lunch preparation really easy, prepare the noodles in the morning, stow the cooked noodles away for the day and then bring the noodles back out at lunch to finish the preparation of this dish.

If you prepare the noodles in the morning, then you will not have to get out a camp kitchen (stove, pots and pans, fuel, etc.) at lunchtime.

4 Servings

1 (8 ounce) package soba noodles*

¾ cup peanut butter

¼ cup + 2 tablespoons apple cider vinegar

1 tablespoon sugar

1 tablespoon minced fresh ginger

1 tablespoon soy sauce

1 clove garlic, peeled and minced*

1 ½ tablespoons lime juice

½ cup chopped cilantro, divided, (optional)

1 English cucumber, peeled, halved and sliced very thin

1 small red bell pepper, sliced thin

2 large carrots, grated

½ cup chopped dry roasted peanuts, (optional)

Morning Prep: cook noodles in boiling salted water according to package directions. Do not overcook. Drain as much water as possible. Store in a secure container until lunchtime.

Lunchtime Prep: mix peanut butter, vinegar, sugar, ginger, soy sauce, garlic, lime juice, and ¼ cup cilantro (optional) until smooth and creamy. Add ¼ cup of water and stir.

Toss together noodles, cucumber, bell pepper, carrots, and peanut butter mixture. If the peanut sauce needs to be thinned, add 1 tablespoon of warm water at a time.

Garnish with remaining cilantro and chopped peanuts.

*Soba Noodles – Soba is a Japanese word for buckwheat. Buckwheat soba noodles have a nutty full-bodied flavor. If you desire the traditional soba noodles check the ingredient list for buckwheat, as some brands add wheat or are even all wheat. I like all the varieties, wheat or buckwheat.

*1 entire clove of raw garlic creates a pretty strong garlic flavor, so you may want to add less depending on your personal taste for garlic.

GORP

Did you know GORP is a Boy Scout acronym for good old raisins and peanuts!

This is my take on the traditional recipe, but I encourage you to experiment with your favorite ingredients. A traditional ratio of 1 to 1 peanuts and raisins is basic and good, for a bit of chocolate sweetness add M&Ms.

8 Servings

    ½ cup cashews pieces

    ½ cup walnuts pieces

    ¼ cup peanuts

    ¼ cup sunflower seeds

    ¾ cup raisins

    ¼ cup dried cranberries

At Home Prep: premix all the ingredients into a large bag to take with you on your adventure.

Did you know?

The first trail "GORP" was invented by the Greek army. In 150 B.C. military officers made pellets mixed with honey (for protein and carbohydrates), opium poppy (to control hunger pains), and a medicinal root called squill (acting as a stimulant). It was considered a good on-the-go snack.

I think I will experiment with that sometime, might be fun to play around with ~ please write to me with your creative GORP discoveries at www.nocoolers.com

Terra's Lunch Couscous

My daughter served this at lunch and I immediately thought, "ah-ha! This would make a great no coolers recipe." It is an easy lunch to prepare, but keep in mind you will need to get out a simple kitchen at lunch time in order to sauté veggies and boil water.

4 Hearty Servings

      3 tablespoons oil

      1 cup sliced green onions, with some of the green top (reserve part of the leaves for topping)

      1 green bell pepper, diced for quick cooking

      1 red bell pepper, diced for quick cooking

      3 cups water

      2 tablespoons soy sauce

      1 teaspoon sugar

      ½ teaspoon ground ginger

      ½ teaspoon garlic powder

      ½ teaspoon ground red pepper

      2 cups couscous

      1 cup dry roasted peanuts (optional)

Sauté diced peppers for about 2 minutes over medium heat, then add onion. Sauté another 3 minutes or until vegetables are soft. Add water, soy sauce, and spices, bring to a boil. Remove from heat, add couscous. Stir and cover, let stand for 5 minutes. Fluff and serve. If you have leftover green onion tops, use them and the nuts as a topper for individual portions of couscous.

Cowboy Caviar

We love to eat this any time, it's fab with Tortilla Chips!

4 Servings

> 1 (15 ounce) can black eye peas or pinto beans, drained and rinsed
>
> 1 (15 ounce) can black beans, drained and rinsed
>
> 1 (15 ounce) can dark red kidney beans, drained and rinsed
>
> 1 (7 ounce) can corn, drained and rinsed
>
> 1 bunch of scallions, sliced cross-ways finely
>
> 1 (7 ounce) can green chilies, diced
>
> 1 small bottle of Italian salad dressing
>
> 1 avocado, diced (optional)
>
> 1 bunch cilantro, chopped (optional)
>
> 1 lime, juiced (optional)
>
> Corn chips or tortillas chips

Drain as much liquid as possible from all cans. Mix contents together. Toss with remaining ingredients. Serve with corn chips or tortillas

Note: only use ½ a bottle of the Italian dressing and ½ can green chilies. Then people can top their individual servings with more dressing and chilies if they prefer.

Variation: also good on top of salads. I love avocado so I prefer to use 2 (or more!). Of course, if you have a favorite home-made Italian dressing, use that in place of the store-bought brands.

APPETIZER~ DAYS 7 TO 12

Days 7 to 12: Quick & Easy – use the following recipes during the second week of a long trip.

Veggies with Peanut Dipping Sauce

A friend of mine likes the Peanut Dipping Sauce so much that she recommends doubling the sauce recipe for added dipping.

4 Servings

⅓ cup water

5 packets True Lime

1 teaspoon garlic powder

1 ½ tablespoons soy sauce

1 ½ tablespoons sugar

3 tablespoons smooth peanut butter

1 teaspoon powdered ginger

¼ teaspoon red pepper flakes

¼ cup vegetable oil

3 cups vegetables of your choice for dipping

Prepare the Sauce: mix ⅓ cup water and True Lime. Add all the sauce ingredients and whisk well to make a smooth sauce. This will take a lot of whisking to combine and emulsify until it is smooth. It is emulsified once the oil and water do not separate.

Chop vegetable for dipping and serve.

Pesto Rounds

Quick, easy and delicious!

4 Servings

> 1 (5 ounce) package crackers of your choice
>
> 10 ounces fresh parmesan cheese
>
> Small tube of pesto paste (Napoleon or Amore brands in a tube)*
>
> Olive oil for drizzling small portions over individual crackers

Place crackers on an appetizing serving plate.

Slice cheese, place on cracker, and squeeze a little bit of pesto paste over cheese. Lastly, drizzle a little bit of olive oil over all.

Variation: if made early in the trip use fresh tomatoes and mozzarella cheese. Slice cheese and tomatoes. Place slices on crackers. Squeeze a small portion of pesto paste onto fresh mozzarella and sliced tomatoes. Lastly, drizzle olive oil over all.

*Fresh basil will not keep without refrigeration so I use Pesto Paste sold in a tube. Amore brand Pesto Paste is a fresh tasting combination of basil, sunflower and olive oils, salt, pine nuts, and garlic. Most grocery stores carry it.

MAIN COURSE ~ DAYS 7 TO 12

Days 7 to 12: Quick & Easy – use the following recipes during the second week of a long trip.

Spaghetti in Marinara Sauce

Everyone loves quick and basic spaghetti. I have spiced this up a little bit with onion, garlic and mushrooms!

4 Servings

> 1 pound spaghetti
>
> 1 (24 ounce) can spaghetti sauce
>
> 1 onion, chopped
>
> 4 cloves garlic, minced
>
> 1 small can mushrooms, sliced
>
> 4 ounces parmesan cheese

As the spaghetti cooks, chop and sauté the onion and garlic. Open cans of sauce and mushrooms. Drain mushrooms and add to translucent onions. Add sauce and simmer as pasta continues to cook.

Drain spaghetti and serve. Divide out 4 plates of pasta and top each plate of spaghetti with sauce and parmesan cheese.

Vegetarian Burrito Bar

As a child I lived in East L.A and was surrounded by Latino families. Many of my recipes have a spicy flare influenced from my childhood.

This recipe is loosely based on a family recipe handed down to us from a lovely neighbor from Mexico. She introduced us to the practice of adding fresh potatoes and carrots to meat tacos.

Now, as a vegetarian I add potatoes, carrots and chilies to my bean burritos. This has been a very popular dinner over the years and is a go-to recipe, made on almost every trip. It is flavorful, simple and modifiable to your particular palate. Add the veggies and chili or leave them out.

I often add more spice and variety by replacing the basil with ancho or other dried chili powder, your choice, play around with the spices to accommodate your taste buds.

4 Servings

> 2 cups refried beans, instant
>
> 3 potatoes, cut in ½ " cubes
>
> 1 ½ carrots, cut in ½ " cubes
>
> ½ onion, chopped
>
> ¾ tablespoon basil
>
> ¼ lettuce
>
> 1 tomato
>
> 1 ½ avocados
>
> ¼ pound cheese, grated
>
> 1 (9 ounce) can salsa

10 flour tortillas, large burrito size

1 can green chilies, diced

1 can crema*

Reconstitute the beans per package directions. Do this first so there is plenty of time for the beans to hydrate.

Chop the carrots, potatoes and onions. Sauté these three vegetables. Once sautéed add basil and toss. Chop the lettuce, tomatoes and avocado.

To Serve: set-out cheese, crema, and canned chilies for a self-serve burrito bar.

*Crema is a delicious light cream. Find it in a can Media Crema Table Cream. Most grocery stores stock it with the canned evaporated milk.

Hoisin Tofu Stir Fry

I loved this dish on the Rio Maranon, aka Grand Canyon of the Amazon, in northern Peru. This is truly an international dish as all of the recipe ingredients for the Rio Maranon trip were purchased at a traditional Peruvian mercado, but for your USA expedition all ingredients can also be found in the average United States supermarket. I have left white space on the following page for you to jot down your recipe personalization notes for future reference. *

4 Servings

⅓ cup Hoisin sauce

2 tablespoons wine

3 tablespoons olive oil (to be divided between the tofu and the vegetables)

1 tablespoon soy sauce

1 pound extra firm tofu, shelf-stable UHT boxed

6 cloves garlic, minced

⅛ teaspoon dried crushed red pepper flakes (more if you like spicey food)

1 red pepper (fresh), cut in to 3 x ½-inch strips

1 whole cauliflower, cut into small florets

½ cup (or less) peanuts, chopped

3 carrots, chopped

⅓ cup water

6 cups cooked rice or couscous or rice noodles

Make Sauce: combine Hoisin and wine in a small bowl and set aside.

Tofu: it is a good idea to press the tofu before slicing (see other tofu recipes for directions on pressing). Cut tofu into 2 by ½ inch slices. Heat about 2 tablespoons of oil in wok or large skillet over high heat until hot but not smoking. Make sure tofu is patted very dry to prevent sticking and splattering oil too much. Add tofu to pan and fry until lightly golden. Transfer tofu to a platter and set aside.

In the same pan cook vegetables with a teaspoon or so of oil. Add garlic, dried crushed pepper flakes, and carrots. Cover and cook for 3 minutes. Stir in fresh red pepper, cauliflower and peanuts and toss to coat with the garlic. Pour in water and soy sauce, cover the pan and cook for about 5 minutes or until vegetable are tender but crunchy.

Stir in tofu, then pour on the Hoisin sauce mixture. Stir fry 1 minute or until the sauce coats everything and is thickened. Serve over rice, or couscous or Thai rice noodles

*Notes for Future Reference

_____

_____

_____

_____

_____

_____

Sweet and Spicy Thai Noodles

Noodles and vegetables are combined in a garden-fresh mix that's a vegetarian delight. Be creative with this recipe making it the correct spiciness for your palate and changing the vegetable to noodle ratios to suit your preference.

4 Servings

Sweet and Spicy Thai Sauce

> 1 ⅓ cups sugar
>
> 1 cup rice vinegar or apple cider vinegar
>
> 1 cup water
>
> 6 cloves garlic, minced or 1 teaspoon garlic powder
>
> ½ to 2 teaspoons crushed red pepper flakes
>
> 2 tablespoons Ultra Gel
>
> 2 tablespoons cold water
>
> 1 teaspoon salt

Noodle Mixture

> 1 (8 ounce) package Thin Thai Rice Noodles
>
> ¼ cup oil
>
> 2 garlic cloves, minced or ¼ teaspoon garlic powder
>
> 1 ½ cups onion, chopped (about 1 small onion)
>
> 4 cups green cabbage, coarsely chopped (about 1 small head)
>
> 4 small carrots, grated

1 cup of the homemade Sweet and Spicy Thai Sauce

½ cup soy sauce

1 ½ cup dry roasted peanuts, chopped

Prepare Thai Sauce: add water, rice vinegar, and sugar to a pot over medium-high heat. When the mixture starts to boil, add the garlic and red pepper flakes. Lower the heat and simmer for another couple of minutes. Cook, stirring constantly, until the mixture reaches desired thickness, about 3-5 minutes. Keep in mind the sauce can be adjusted to your preference, can add more water (1 tablespoon at a time) if want it thinner or more thickener if desire it thicker.

Bring large pot of water to boil. Add rice noodles; cook 3 to 5 minutes or until noodles are tender but firm. Rinse under cold water; drain well. Set aside.

Heat oil in large skillet or wok on medium-high heat. Add garlic; stir fry 30 seconds or until fragrant. Add onion; stir fry 2 minutes or until onion softens. Add cabbage, carrots, soy sauce and 1 cup of homemade Thai Sauce; stir fry 3 to 5 minutes or until cabbage is tender-crisp. Add rice noodles; stir fry 3 to 4 minutes.

Top each individual serving with peanuts. If you have extra sauce, serve it on the side.

This dish is good with tofu on the side as well, see the Crunchy Salt Cured Tofu recipe.

Papas a la Huancaina con Arroz

The recipe name translated into English means potatoes in a chili pepper cheese sauce with rice.

This is a delicious Peruvian dish, but when made from scratch in Peru it contains soft fresh cheese which is not practical with the no coolers camp kitchen philosophy because that type of cheese is not possible without a cooler and ice, but I have a solution!

One of the tricks is to purchase the pre-made Huancaina sauce, see the description at the end of this recipe to learn more about Huancaina. You will have to do a bit of a search to find this product because it is imported from Peru, but it is worth the purchase. I keep this product in my home kitchen as well because it is an easy way to dress-up potatoes and make a variety of casseroles.

4 Servings

> 4 eggs, hard boiled
>
> 4 large yellow potatoes
>
> 1 (4 ounce) can sliced black olives
>
> 3 tablespoons stick margarine
>
> 1 small onion, chopped
>
> 2 cloves garlic, minced
>
> 2 (14 ounce) Huancaina (Peruvian packages, which come as 400 g portions)*
>
> 2 cups instant rice (arroz)

Place eggs in a separate pot, cover with water bring to a boil, boil for 1 minute and take off flame, let set. Cook instant rice, follow directions on package, and set aside.

Peel and cut potatoes in half, place potatoes in a pan and cover with an inch of water. Place lid on pan and bring to boil. Remove lid and turn to simmer and cook for about 15 minutes (do not overcook). Remove potatoes from hot water.

Chop onion and mince garlic. Sauté garlic and onions. Add Huancaina sauce to sauté pan, stir in a little bit of water at a time until it is the consistency you like, set aside.

Once potatoes are cool enough to handle, slice the potatoes into thick slices and cut the eggs in half.

To Serve: reheat Huancaina sauce. Place papas (potatoes) on individual plates, with egg halves, pour a about ¼ cup of Huancaina sauce on each serving of potatoes and lightly sprinkle with olives. Serve with rice on the side with some Huancaina sauce.

*Huancaina Sauce is a popular and traditional Peruvian sauce for potatoes. Common name is yellow hot chili cheese sauce. The homemade version is very basic, made from Aji peppers, fresh soft cheese and saltine crackers. The recipe in this cookbook uses a prepackaged sauce which is a product of Peru. It is very hard to find this sauce in USA grocery stores, but Amazon has it. Order the Alacena brand; the name is Huancaina, but you may need to look for it under the full name, Crema de aji y queso Huancaina Receta Casera. It comes in a handy durable bag.

Dreamy Sauce Pasta

For a little spicy kick, add a pinch or more of cayenne pepper.

4 Servings

    1 (10 ounce can) stewed tomatoes, undrained

    1 cup crema

    1 tablespoon oil

    3 cloves garlic

    ½ cup Kraft parmesan cheese*

    ½ pound pasta shells (8 ounce boxed)

    ½ to 1 tablespoon dried basil, optional

    6 ounces fresh parmesan cheese (for on the side and optional)

    Cayenne pepper, optional

As the pasta is cooking, peel and finely chop the garlic. In large pot sauté the garlic with oil. Turn down heat to medium flame. Add undrained canned tomatoes (do not drain) and basil. Add the crema. Add ½ cup Kraft parmesan cheese and basil (to taste) to the crema mixture. Low simmer for about 2 minutes over medium heat, melt cheese, stirring frequently.

Drain the pasta, add to the sauce. If too thick add a little bit of water. If using fresh parmesan cheese, grate set aside.

To serve: reheat as needed. Set out fresh parmesan and cayenne pepper to sprinkle on individual servings. Salt and pepper as desired.

116

SIDE DISH ~ DAYS 7 TO 12

Days 7 to 12: Quick & Easy – use the following recipes during the second week of a long trip.

Garlic Brown Rice

Instant brown rice is healthier than the white rice variety. Most grocery stores carry it.

4 Servings

> 1 ⅓ cups instant brown rice
>
> 1 ⅔ cups water
>
> ¼ teaspoon garlic powder
>
> ⅓ teaspoon dried garlic, minced
>
> 2 tablespoons dried minced onion
>
> ½ cube vegetable bouillon
>
> ¼ cup freeze-dried corn – can substitute with canned or dehydrated corn*
>
> ¼ cup freeze-dried peas – can substitute with canned or dehydrated peas*

Place vegetables and spices in cool water. Cover and bring to a boil. Stir in rice, return to boil. Turn to low, cover and simmer for 5 minutes. Remove from heat. Let stand for at least 15 minutes, fluff and serve.

*If using dehydrated corn or peas reconstitute longer. Let the water boil dehydrated vegetables a little longer as well as set to rehydrate a little longer, before adding rice.

Tex-Mex Rice

This rice complements a variety of meals and has just a bit of spicy kick.

4 Servings

   ¾ cup long-grain rice

   2 tablespoons oil

   ½ cup carrots, fresh and chopped

   1 (5.5 ounce) V-8 (spicey V-8 if you like it hot)

   ½ teaspoon garlic powder

   1 teaspoon mild chili powder – like ancho or pasilla

   ¼ teaspoon salt

   1 tablespoon dried onion (diced or minced)

   1 ¾ cup vegetable broth (1 ¾ cups water with 1 vegetable bouillon cube)

   ½ cup canned corn

   3 tablespoons canned peas

In a larger fry pan, lightly brown rice and fresh carrots in oil over med-high heat. Stir often to avoid sticking. Add tomato juice and cook for 5 minutes on low heat, stirring. Stir in broth, garlic and chili powder, and salt over medium heat. When rice begins to boil, turn heat to low, cover and cook for about 20 minutes (add water if absorbed before 20 minutes). Remove from heat add corn and peas. Let rest for 5 minutes, fluff and serve.

Creamy Carrot Slaw

I make this on almost every trip.

4 Servings

  2 whole large carrots, grated

  1 ½ whole oranges

  2 tablespoons sunflower seeds

  ½ tablespoon sugar

  ½ carton crema

  2 tablespoons raisins

Grate the carrots, chop up 2 of the oranges and squeeze the third one over the mixture. Add everything else and toss. It is up to you as to how "wet" you want this salad. The more crema and orange juice, the wetter.

Sweet and Sour Fruit Salad

For no-mess prep clean-up, mix in a large zip top freezer bag.

4 Servings

  1 (15 ounce) can mandarin orange segments in light syrup

  1 lemon

  ¼ cup raisins

  ¼ cup walnuts, chopped

  2 apples

Chop the apples, open and drain the mandarin oranges.

In a bowl mix the fruit with raisins and juice from the lemon. Add the walnuts.

Garlic Bread

It may seem strange that this garlic bread recipe calls for hot dog buns, let me explain.

"Back in the day," I remember searching all over the small pueblo of Sahuaripa, Mexico. There were a few tiendas (small grocery stores), but no supermarkets. Our rafting party was securing the last bits of the food supply. We were about to embark on a 12-day river expedition on the Rio Mulatos, Aros and Yaqui. I was intent on finding French bread or something similar for my garlic bread recipe. It was nowhere to be found so I ended up buying the closest thing I could find – hot dog buns!

Since that long-ago date I have been hired as a camp chef in many parts of the world (Mexico, Guatemala, Peru and the USA). In the more exotic locals, I have not been able to find French bread, but I can always find hot dog buns. Turns out hot dog buns will last a very long time; they will still be good even into the second or third week of a river expedition!

4 Servings

> 4 white hot dog buns (or ½ loaf French bread)
>
> 6 tablespoons sick margarine (3/8 cup)
>
> 4 to 6 cloves garlic, minced

Melt margarine in a saucepan and add the garlic and maybe some basil if you like. Blend together.

Split the buns in half lengthwise. Spread the garlic/margarine over the halves of bread and toast on a griddle or skillet over med heat until golden brown.

Slice and serve.

Southwest Quinoa

Wonderfully light, healthy and nutritious.

4 Servings

    1 tablespoon olive oil

    2 cloves garlic, minced

    1 jalapeno, minced

    1 cup quinoa

    1 cup water

    1 (15-ounce) can black beans, drained

    1 (14.5 ounce) can diced tomatoes

    1 (8 ounce) can corn, drained

    1 teaspoon ancho chili powder

    ½ teaspoon cumin

    1 avocado, peeled and diced

    1 lime, juiced

    Bag of tortilla chips

Heat olive oil in a large skillet over medium high heat. Add garlic and jalapeno, cook, about 1 minute.

Stir in quinoa, water, beans, tomatoes, corn, chili powder and cumin; season with salt and pepper, to taste. Bring to a boil; cover, reduce heat and simmer until quinoa is cooked through, about 20 minutes.

In a separate bowl squeeze lime over avocado season with salt to taste. Serve in individual bowls topped with avocado and a handful or tortilla chips on the side

Chayotes Fritos

Chayote is a type of squash native to the Americas. It grows profusely in Mexico and is common in USA. It is a small, hard and mild flavored squash that retains a bit of firmness even when cooked. It is a versatile vegetable that can be eaten raw, boiled, fried and added to any dish because it takes on the flavor of what it is cooked with.

Serves 4

2 chayotes, peeled, pitted and thinly sliced*

3 tablespoons stick margarine

1 medium onion, sliced

½ teaspoon salt

¼ teaspoon pepper

Heat the margarine in a large skillet over medium heat until margarine is melted. Add the onions and sauté until they are golden, but not browned, about 8 minutes. Add the chayote and continue cooking until softens, about 4 minutes. Lower the heat and cover. Let simmer for about 10 minutes until the chayote squash is soft and onions browned.

Remove from heat, add salt and pepper, toss and serve warm.

*Chayotes: when peeling chayote be sure to remove all of the outside skin, even into the folds, as the skin sometimes has an unusual fuzzy film on it that does not wash off.

DESSERT ~ DAYS 7 TO 12

Days 7 to 12: Quick & Easy – use the following recipes during the second week of a long trip.

Chocolate Sea Salt Almonds

A chocolate treat to feel good about! Save this recipe for those cool weather trips, as chocolate tends to melt in hot climates.

Yields: 1 ¼ cup almonds

 ½ tablespoon coconut oil

 1 cup semi-sweet chocolate chips

 1 ¼ cups whole almonds

 Sea salt or Kosher salt

 Turbinado sugar or any coarse sugar

Set out wax or parchment paper. Melt the chocolate in a double boiler. Stir the almonds into the chocolate; completely coat with chocolate. Remove with spoon or fork. Set on wax paper. Sprinkle with sea salt and coarse sugar.

Let set for an hour or so. How quickly they harden will depend on the air temperature.

Ginger Tea with Pineapple Slices

This recipe is elegant, simple, and delicious.

This fresh ginger tea recipe came from a friend while sharing meal responsibilities on a Colorado River Grand Canyon trip. She prepared the tea on our 18-day private cost-shared expedition.

It was our night to do the cooking and we were lacking a dessert. My friend searched in the group food supply box and was delighted to find fresh ginger because she said she made fresh ginger tea at home all the time.

I like sugar coated dried pineapples, but they are a bit sweet for eating on their own. Fresh ginger tea cuts the sugar and adds a complex flavor combination I enjoy very much. This makes a fine dessert.

4 Servings

> 8 (more or less) sugar-coated dehydrated pineapple rings
>
> 4 inches (more or less) of ginger root
>
> 2 quarts of water
>
> Honey or agave nectar
>
> Orange peel (optional)

Cut the ginger root into chunks. Place in water. Bring to a boil and boil for about 10 minutes. Remove from heat and let steep for a few minutes. Sweeten to taste with honey or agave nectar.

Serve the pineapple as a snack to eat with the tea.

Variation: even tastier with a bit of orange peel added to the tea as it cooks and steeps.

124

Nut Fudge

If there are any leftovers, set them out in the morning for a sweet treat with breakfast.

Yields: 24 tablespoon-sized cookies

> ½ cup honey
>
> ¼ cup unsweetened cocoa powder
>
> ¼ cup coconut oil
>
> ½ cup peanut butter
>
> ¼ teaspoon salt
>
> ¾ cup sunflower seeds, dry roasted
>
> 1 ¼ cups peanuts, dry roasted, salted, chopped

This fudge can set up rapidly, so it is best to have all ingredients measured and ready. Set out wax paper.

In a saucepan over medium heat, combine the honey, cocoa powder, and coconut oil. Stir until all is melted. The mixture will be very thick. Allow to boil for about 1 minute. Remove from heat and stir in peanut butter and salt until completely smooth.

Add the sunflower seeds and peanuts, mixing well to make sure the nuts are well coated with the chocolate/peanut butter mixture. Using a spoon, drop mixture into small piles on way paper.

S'mores Rice Krispies Treats

Your favorite campfire treats without the campfire. If there are any leftovers, set them out in the morning because these treats are good with morning coffee!

Yields: 24 Squares

> 6 cups Rice Krispies Cereal
>
> 1 bag (10.5-ounce) miniature marshmallows
>
> 1/4 cup stick margarine + 1 tablespoon for pan
>
> 1 1/2 cups (4 ounces) graham cracker pieces
>
> 1 1/4 cups semi-sweet chocolate chips

Spread 1 tablespoon of margarine in the bottom and sides of pan, so krispies do not stick to pan. Use an 11x7 dish or any other camping pan that you think will work. Set aside.

In a large saucepan, melt the margarine. Pour in the marshmallows and constantly stir until melted.

Remove the pan from heat and pour in the Rice Krispies cereal and graham cracker pieces. Quickly mix together well.

Add 1 cup chocolate chips and gently stir - you want most of the chips to hold their shape and not to completely melt.

Immediately place the rice krispie treats into prepared baking pan. Top the treats with remaining 1/4 cup chocolate chips and press hard and flatten rice krispie treats.

It will take about half hour for the treats to cool. Cut into squares.

Chocolate Walnuts

So simple, so good! Best to make this dessert during cooler weather trips, as chocolate tends to melt in hot summer climates without ice and a cooler.

As a child, my Grampa loved chocolate covered walnuts, but then the Great Depression hit and him and family were forced into a severe financial budget that would not allow for luxury food items. In fact, I remember his stories about subsisting on only crackers and ketchup – but I digress. Back to the history of this chocolate walnuts recipe.

After their marriage, when Gramma discovered Grampa loved these treats, she taught herself how to make them. This saved them money (as the depression was over but they still valued a budget). I hope you too enjoy this home-made candy!

Yields: 1 ¼ cup of nuts

      1 cup semi-sweet chocolate chips

      ½ tablespoon coconut oil

      1 ¼ cup walnuts, halves

Use a double boiler to melt chocolate chips. If do not have a double boiler, set a smaller pot with the chips in a larger pot filled with water and bring to a boil. Completely melt chocolate, add the coconut oil, and stir well. Drop in whole walnuts to coat them completely. Carefully lift walnuts out of chocolate and drop on wax paper.

Let set for an hour or so. How quickly the chocolate sets and hardens will depend on the air temperature.

~~~~~~

WEEK 3
DAYS 13 TO 18

~ EFFORTLESS & CAREFREE ~

Use the recipes in this section during the third week
of a long trip.

The ingredients in the recipes for days 13 through 18
will last into the third week of an 18-Day journey
because they are nonperishable. The recipe
ingredients consist of longer-lasting fresh vegetables,
freeze-dried items, dehydrated foods and canned
goods.

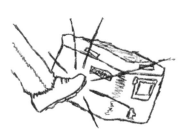

Kick the Cooler Habit!

~~~~~~

BREAKFAST ~ DAYS 13 TO 18

Fast Blueberry Quinoa

Great with a variety of toppings, such as: honey, maple syrup, fresh fruit, raisins, nuts, granola, chia seeds, etc. Also good with alternative milks, like: coconut, rice, soy, etc.

4 Servings

> 1 ½ cups quinoa flakes*
>
> 6 cups water
>
> 1 cup powdered milk
>
> 2 ¼ cups freeze-dried blueberries
>
> 3 tablespoons of sugar or another sweetener
>
> Pinch of salt

In saucepan set on medium heat bring the water and dried blueberries to a boil and turn off immediately (do not cook blueberries too long they will disintegrate).

Remove water and blueberries from the flame and add the quinoa flakes, powdered milk sugar and salt. Give the cereal a stir. Let cereal sit for 3 minutes.

Give a final stir, serve and add toppings.

*Quinoa flakes are made by Ancient Harvest; you can find this brand in some markets and online.

Western Scramble

Dehydrated Shredded Potatoes are the key to success; I like the Hungry Jack brand of Original Hash Brown Potatoes. Most grocery stores carry them, look for them in a small square carton on the shelf, not in the refrigerator case.

4 Servings

> 1 (4.2 ounce) dehydrated shredded potatoes (Hungry Jack Hash Brown Potatoes)
>
> 1 tablespoon dried mixed bell pepper (Harmony House)
>
> ¼ teaspoon dried minced garlic
>
> ½ tablespoon dried minced onion
>
> 1 (2 ounce) packet powdered egg mix (OvaEasy Egg Crystals is a good brand)
>
> ¾ cup + 2 tablespoons water for the eggs
>
> 3 tablespoons oil
>
> ¼ cup Kraft dried parmesan cheese (optional)
>
> ¼ cup soy bacon bits (optional)
>
> Pinch of cayenne (optional)

Prior Evening Prep: boil a large pot of water (about 1 quart). Place dried potatoes, peppers, garlic and onion in the pot. Pour in enough hot water to cover. Soak overnight.

Morning Prep: drain the potato mixture, let drain for a few minutes and press to remove water. Place potatoes on a clean dishtowel to dry (get them as dry as possible).

Reconstitute the dried eggs in water. In a bowl whisk 7/8 cups water and entire 2-ounce package of eggs (½ cup egg powder) until thoroughly mixed. Set aside.

Preheat 3 tablespoons oil in a large, non-stick skillet over medium-high heat. Spread potato mixture evenly. Cook for 6 minutes, stirring thoroughly every 2 minutes. Brown the last 2 minutes. After 6 minutes add egg mixture, cover pan and let cook a minute, until egg is done.

Serve with the optional parmesan cheese, soy bacon bits and for a bit of zip, cayenne pepper. Salt and pepper to taste. And of course, the Spiced Hot Apples!

Spiced Hot Apples

1 (4 ounce) package dried apples, slices

½ teaspoon cinnamon

⅓ cup brown sugar

Pinch ground cloves

Pinch ground nutmeg

Prior Evening Prep: boil a large pot of water. Place apples, cinnamon, cloves, nutmeg, and brown sugar in a pot. Pour just enough of the hot water to cover apples. Soak overnight.

Morning Prep: bring the apples to a boil and simmer for 15 minutes, covered, set aside after 15 minutes (watch, may need to add water, keep from scorching).

Set aside, to be served with the Western Scramble.

Quinoa de Canela

Unlike wheat or rice, quinoa contains a balanced set of essential amino acids, making it a complete protein. Quinoa is gluten-free and is considered easy to digest.

4 Servings

> 1 cup quinoa
>
> 2 cups water for cooking quinoa
>
> 2 heaping teaspoons brown sugar
>
> 1 tablespoon cinnamon, ground (canela in Spanish)
>
> 1 tablespoon coconut oil (or other fat)
>
> 2 tablespoons dried cranberries
>
> ¼ cup chia seeds, optional
>
> ½ cup dry whole milk powder (NIDO)
>
> 1 ¼ cups water for reconstituting milk

Add quinoa, water, brown sugar, canela (cinnamon), coconut oil, and cranberries to a pan and bring to a boil.

Reduce to a simmer, cover, and cook until all the water is absorbed (about 15 minutes). You will know the quinoa is done when the whitish spiral-like germ has separated.

As quinoa cooks reconstitute the milk. Add the water amount listed above for reconstituting the milk to the milk powder and mix thoroughly. The quinoa is very good with about ½ cup milk per serving bowl.

Top with chia seeds if desired.

Breakfast Buffet for Nomads

I like this breakfast buffet so much; I make it at home too!

4 Servings

Cereal Mix

> 1 cup granola
>
> 1 cup Grape-Nuts cereal
>
> 1 cup freeze-dried blueberries
>
> 5 tablespoons almonds slivered or chopped
>
> 2 tablespoons hazelnuts chopped
>
> ⅓ cup macadamia nuts chopped
>
> 1 tablespoon vanilla powder

Buffet Items

> ¼ cup chia seeds
>
> ¼ cup Cacao Nibs
>
> ¼ cup dried cranberries or raisins
>
> ¼ cup semi-sweet chocolate chips
>
> ⅓ cup dry whole milk powder (NIDO)
>
> 8 prepackaged fruit fill breakfast bars

At Home Prep: mix granola, Grape Nuts, freeze-dried blueberries, slivered almonds, hazelnuts, macadamia nuts and vanilla powder. Place in a sturdy plastic freezer bags or other sturdy container.

To Serve: set out bag of Cereal Mix and all other items buffet style. The fruit filled breakfast bars are for guests to eat alongside personalized cereal or later in the day.

River Ranger Oats

While doing multi-day river patrols in Canyonlands National Park on the Green and Colorado Rivers this was one of my go-to breakfasts, fast and filling!

4 Servings

> 2 cups instant oatmeal
>
> ⅓ cup raisins
>
> ⅓ cup walnuts, chopped
>
> ½ cup brown sugar
>
> ¼ teaspoon cinnamon
>
> ¼ teaspoon nutmeg
>
> ¾ cup dry whole milk powder (NIDO)
>
> 3 ½ cups water

Bring water to a boil. Add all ingredients. Let set with lid on for about 2 minutes, stir and serve

River Ranger Reminder for Leave No Trace:
1. *Plan ahead and prepare*
2. *Travel and camp on durable surfaces*
3. *Dispose of waste water properly*
4. *Leave what you find*
5. *Minimize campfire impacts, be very careful with fire*
6. *Respect wildlife*
7. *Be considerate of other visitors*

LUNCH ~ DAYS 13 TO 18

Day 13 to 18: Effortless & Carefree – use the following recipes during the third week of a long trip.

Eastern Hummus Wraps

The Eastern Hummus Wraps are good served with the Spiced Jicama Sticks and GORP

Dried powdered hummus is an amazing kitchen item for the vegetarian following a no coolers philosophy. It is easy to prepare, tasty, nutritious and non-perishable. Did you know that hummus is made from chickpeas (Garbanzo beans) which are high in protein, perfect for a vegetarian or vegan!

Yields: 1 ½ cups Hummus

> ¾ cup instant hummus
>
> ¼ teaspoon mild curry powder
>
> ¼ teaspoon ginger powder
>
> ¾ cup freeze-dried mangoes*
>
> 2 tablespoons olive oil
>
> 1 cup water
>
> 1 package of Flatbread (large tortillas work too)

For easy prep and clean-up, place the dry ingredients into the zip top bag. Add the water, oil, freeze-dried mangoes and spices. Squeeze out any excess air and securely close the bag top, then very carefully knead to blend all ingredients.

Spread the hummus on the bread and roll (depending on the typed of bread you have).

*Freeze-dried mangoes - The freeze-dried mangoes can be replaced with dehydrated mangoes, which most grocery stores carry. For dehydrated mangoes use only ⅔ cup, chopped.

Black Bean Corn Salad

Just boil for a savory vegetarian friendly "salad" using dried ingredients.

4 Servings

> 1 cup dried black beans (Mother Earth Products)
>
> ¾ cup freeze-dried corn
>
> 2 tablespoons dried tomatoes
>
> 2 tablespoons dried minced onion
>
> 2 (7 ounce) cans Jalapenos in Escabeche, sliced (Herdez brand is good)
>
> 2 (7 ounce) cans Crema
>
> 1 (10 ounce) bag tortilla chips or Mexican Tostados (see Ingredient Notes) or Frito-Lay Tostidos

Morning Prep: place beans, corn, tomatoes, onion in a large pot. Drain and save the Escabeche juice from the can of jalapenos. In a separate bowl add enough water to the jalapeno Escabeche to make 3 cups of liquid. Add this flavorful "juice" to the beans, corn, tomatoes and onions, stir. Bring to a boil and set aside. Once cooled place in a spill proof container to sit and rehydrate for about 4 hours.

Lunchtime Prep: cut up about 2 tablespoons of the jalapenos and carrots from the jalapenos in Escabeche. Add to beans and mix well.

Before serving you may want to drain the beans of excess water. Serve with extra jalapenos, Crema and tortilla chips on the side.

Italian Couscous Buffet

This can be a versatile recipe and one to adjust to your group's palate. Make this dish nomad style (using no coolers and all nonperishable ingredients) or if recipe is made early in a trip, turn it into a buffet style salad; using fresh produce.

4 Servings

Couscous Mixture

> 1 ⅓ cup couscous
>
> ½ cup Knorr instant vegetable soup
>
> 2 tablespoons dried mixed peppers
>
> ¼ cup Parmesan cheese (Kraft grated works well) + extra for topping
>
> ½ cup walnuts
>
> 2 ounces dried tomatoes (about ⅔ cup loosely packed
>
> 2 ⅓ cup water hot water
>
> 4 hard-boiled eggs (quartered and optional)
>
> 1 cup high quality balsamic vinegar (drizzle for optional topping)
>
> 1 cup olive oil (drizzle for optional topping)

Morning Prep: place couscous, Knorr soup, parmesan cheese, tomatoes and walnuts in a pot, stir to mix, add the hot water. Stir, remove from flame and cover. Once cooled, place in a secure container to store all day without spilling. Bring out for final prep at lunchtime. Also cook (hard boil) eggs in morning.

138

Lunchtime Prep: stir and fluff couscous. Serve with the hard-boiled eggs, additional parmesan cheese, salt and pepper. I like to drizzle a bit of olive oil and good quality balsamic vinegar on top. Each person can adjust to their palate.

Variation: turn the couscous into a more of a salad dish. Use the fresh ingredients below as makings for a salad topper. Make the couscous per directions above and then set out the following fresh produce buffet style.

  2 carrots, grated

  2 celery, diced

  1 small jicama, diced

  1 cup romaine lettuce, shredded

  1 cup Napa cabbage, shredded

  2 Roma tomatoes, diced

  2 lemons or limes, quartered

  Italian seasoning

  Fresh parmesan cheese, slivered

In individual bowls scoop up ½ cup couscous, top with fresh vegetables and add toppings of choice - parmesan cheese, vinegar, olive oil, salt and pepper, juice of fresh lemons, fresh parmesan cheese and Italian seasoning.

Quinoa Tabouli

I have replaced the tradition wheat bulgur with quinoa, thus making a gluten-free tabouli. If you make this tabouli on one of the first days of the trip it can become the main ingredient of a healthy fresh salad (see Variation below).

4 Servings

> 1 cup quinoa
>
> 2 cups water for quinoa
>
> 1 tablespoon dried minced onions
>
> ½ tablespoon dried minced garlic
>
> ⅓ cup raisins
>
> ½ cup dried tomatoes, julienne cut*
>
> 1 teaspoon True Lemon*
>
> 3 tablespoons olive oil
>
> ¼ cup sunflower seeds (optional)
>
> Pinch of salt

Morning Prep: prewash quinoa if needed it is not a prewashed brand. Bring the quinoa, dried onion and garlic to boil. Reduce to simmer, cover. Cook about 15 minutes, until water is absorbed. Once cooled place in a container that will not leak throughout the day, to be brought out at lunchtime to finish the preparation of the recipe.

Lunchtime Prep: gently toss quinoa, add raisins and tomatoes. Reconstitute the True Lemon or Lime in 2 tablespoons of water, stir well. With a fork, mix in reconstituted lemon juice, olive oil and a pinch of salt. Re-toss well.

Serve with the remaining tomatoes, sunflower seeds, extra raisins, a shaker of True Lemon or Lime and salt on the side. Each person can adjust the additions to their palate.

Variation: make this recipe early in a trip for a fresher version. To substitute the dried for fresh follow these guidelines: 4 green onions, sliced; 2 Roma tomatoes, diced; fresh garlic minced. Squeeze the juice of 1 to 4 lemons and lastly top with fresh parsley and mint.

*Dried Tomato: in this recipe I prefer the brand California Sun Dry Tomatoes with Herbs in a glass jar. These are these are the softest and most flavorful. Purchase an 8.5-ounce jar in order for there to be extra on the side.

*True Lemon and Lime – A 100% natural product; it is made from lemons and limes. Cold pressing and crystallizing the lemons locks in the great flavor and nutrients.

Trail Lunch for Nomads

Great for a busy day. This is my go-to lunch for a day when people want to keep being active (hiking, rowing, climbing, etc.) through lunchtime or when your group simply does not want to stop and take the time for the traditional lunch.

I set-out the lunch items (buffet style) right after breakfast.

First hand out the individual containers and then people can fill the container with the items listed below. Once done selecting, each person secures their individual lunch packages. They can then be eaten at the time that the individual decides is best. Be it while they are rowing, paddling, hiking, etc. and whenever they prefer to eat lunch throughout the day.

4 Servings

> 8 (1.15 ounce) nut butter spread packets, (Justin's Nut Butter)
>
> 13 ounces of crackers (your choice)
>
> 6 ounces dried fruit
>
> 8 energy bars
>
> 10 ounces cookies (optional)
>
> GORP (recipe on page 99)
>
> 4 baggies or containers for each person

Hand out individual baggies or containers so that each guest can assemble their own lunch.

Lay all items out and guests can prepare their own "bagged" lunches.

APPETIZER ~ DAYS 13 TO 18

Days 13 to 18: Effortless & Carefree – use the following recipes during the third week of a long trip.

Mexico Jicama Sticks

Have you visited Mexico? If so, have you ever wondered what the street vendor is selling. You know, the vendor with the white vegetable sticks sprinkled with a crimson-colored spice; well, this is jicama. Vendors commonly sell jicama with lime juice squeezed over it then sprinkled with a variety of powdered chilies and sometimes a dash of salt.

4 Servings

> 1 large Jicama
>
> 1 lemon or lime
>
> ¼ to ½ teaspoon paprika (mild spice), Ancho Chili powder (med heat), cayenne pepper (spicy), or any combination of spices
>
> Pinch of salt

Peel the jicama and cut jicama into julienne strips (like French fries). Squeeze the juice of the lemon or lime over jicama and sprinkle lightly with your choice of spice (paprika, ancho chili powder, or cayenne pepper or a combo of the three) and a pinch of salt.

Corn and Pepper Soup

This soup comes together very quickly. I love freeze-dried corn; it is even good eaten right out of the package.

4 Servings

    1 cup freeze-dried or dried corn

    ⅓ cup mixed dried peppers (harmony house)

    4 cups water

    ½ teaspoon sugar

    ½ teaspoon salt

    ⅔ teaspoon black pepper

    ⅓ cup dry whole milk powder (NIDO)

    ¼ cup Ultra Gel

    1 cup water

Combine corn, mixed dried peppers, and water in a large pot. Cover pot and bring to a boil. Low simmer for 10 minutes. After 10 minutes add milk powder, sugar, salt, and pepper and stir to mix.

Combine the Ultra Gel and ½ cup of water. Blend with fork so there are no lumps and then add to chowder in order to thicken. If you would like it thinner or would like more chowder add more water a little at a time. Reheat, let sit for a minute then serve.

MAIN COURSE ~ DAYS 13 TO 18

Days 13 to 18: Effortless & Carefree – use the following recipes during the third week of a long trip.

Creamy Lemony Pasta

This recipe is best with the Chayote included, give it a try!

4 Servings

> 1 pound spaghetti
>
> 2 chayote (optional, but really tasty!)
>
> 2 tablespoons salt for spaghetti water
>
> ½ tablespoon True Lemon
>
> ½ cup water for True Lemon
>
> ¼ cup olive oil*
>
> ½ cup Kraft parmesan cheese + extra for side
>
> 1 tablespoon dried basil
>
> 1 (7.6 ounce) can Crema

Remove skin and seed from chayote, slice thin and then in half. Add chayote to spaghetti water. Bring water to a boil in a large pot. Add salt. Follow directions on spaghetti package to cook to desired firmness.

Prepare True Lime "juice." In a large fry pan stir in olive oil, cheese, basil and Crema. Heat on medium flame. Add drained spaghetti with chayote to sauce and stir well. If you would like a thinner sauce add water a little bit at a time until you have the consistency you prefer.

Sweet Potato Quinoa Buffet

Yummy, Yummy, Yummy and Vegan!

4 Servings

Tofu:

>1 or 2 (12 ounce) blocks extra firm tofu in shelf-stable UHT box. Prepare the Crunchy Garlic Tofu (directions on the following pages)

Quinoa:

>2 tablespoons olive oil
>
>1 cup quinoa
>
>2 cups water
>
>1 cube vegetable bouillon (optional)
>
>2 tablespoons soy sauce
>
>1 clove garlic, finely chopped or grated
>
>1 tablespoon ginger, finely chopped or grated

Sweet Potatoes:

>2 medium sized sweet potatoes, peeled, cubed

Serve with:

>1 (7 ounce) bottle Hoisin Sauce or other sauce

First prepare the tofu. Follow directions for the Crunchy Garlic Tofu on the following page.

Prepare the quinoa. Heat olive oil in medium saucepan. Add quinoa and toast for about 2 minutes, stirring occasionally. Add water (with the optional bouillon cube if desired), soy sauce, garlic and ginger. Bring to a boil. Cover and simmer on low heat until broth is absorbed, about 20 minutes.

As the quinoa is cooking prepare the sweet potatoes. Three options for preparation. Fry, steam or boil the cubed sweet potatoes. Either method will take about 20 minutes.

Cut the Hoisin sauce with water or red wine until you have the desired consistency. Set aside.

To Serve: each person receives a large bowl. Fill the bottom of bowl with some quinoa. Top the quinoa with sweet potatoes and tofu. Finally pour the desired amount of Hoisin sauce over all.

Crunchy Garlic Tofu

Start preparing the tofu about 1 hour before the main meal. It is critical to press the tofu to remove excess water for frying.

1 (12 ounce) block extra firm tofu, shelf-stable UHT boxed

¼ cup flour

2 teaspoons garlic powder

1 tablespoon dried minced garlic

½ teaspoon salt

½ teaspoon pepper

2 tablespoons olive oil for frying

The essence of pressing tofu is to apply steady weight to squeeze out the moisture from the tofu block. Be gentle, do not apply too much weight or the tofu will be crushed and you will be unable to cut it into slices.

Instructions for pressing:

Fold a length of paper towels or a dishcloth in half or quarters to increase the absorbency. Place the folded towels on the cutting board (or plate), then place the block of tofu on the paper towels.

Place the weight into the bowl or onto the cutting board (or second plate). Your weight should be heavy enough to press down evenly across the top of the tofu, but not so heavy as to cause the tofu block to crumble. A large canned food item will work.

Let the tofu sit for at least 30 minutes. The weight will gradually and effectively squeeze the moisture out of the block of tofu, where it will be absorbed by the paper towels or dishcloth.

If the paper towels become saturated, you could replace them with fresh paper towels. Continue pressing until the paper towels stop absorbing moisture. After 30 minutes, or no moisture is left, you can proceed to cut the tofu block into strips or cubes for use in recipes.

Preparing the tofu for frying

Slice the tofu into 1/2-inch cubes or slices or both.

Combine dry ingredients in a bowl. Toss the tofu very gently in the flour mixture to coat the tofu well.

In a large skillet, heat the oil over medium heat, once oil is hot, add the tofu. Cook for 4 to 6 minutes, turning occasionally, until outside is golden brown and lightly crispy. Set tofu aside (on paper towel to absorb excess oil) until stir-fries or salads are ready to be topped or tossed with the tofu.

Tamarindo Fried Rice

This recipe was inspired by a traditional Peruvian dish that I modified for this "Nomad" version full of nonperishable ingredients. While living in Peru this was one of my favorite dishes, but it is difficult to find tamarind pulp in the USA, so I made up my own version with easy to find ingredients.

Traditional tamarindo sauce is made from tamarind pulp. The Tamarind tree produces a pod-like fruit that contains an edible pulp. It originates from Africa but is now found in cuisines all over the world (but not much in the USA diet). By itself the flavor is very strong; it has a sweet tart and sometimes very sour taste. Normally the flavors are mellowed by diluting with other ingredients, adding spice (heat), citrus juices, or adding a bit of sweetener

4 Servings

Dried mushroom vegetable mixture

> 1 ounce sliced dried shitake mushroom*
>
> 1 tablespoon minced dried onion
>
> ½ tablespoon minced dried garlic
>
> ¼ cup dried peppers harmony house pepper mix

Rice mixture

> 2 cups instant rice.
>
> 1 large sweet potato (camote)
>
> 2 tablespoons oil
>
> 2 teaspoons ground ginger
>
> 3 tablespoons soy sauce

Egg mixture

> ½ cup Ova Easy eggs (2 ounce package, dried)
>
> 2 tablespoons dry whole milk powder (NIDO)
>
> ¾ cup water

Faux Tamarindo Sauce

> 2 teaspoon true lime
>
> ¼ cup water
>
> 2 tablespoon brown sugar

Morning Prep: add dried shitake mushrooms, dried onion, dried garlic and dried peppers to a pot, cover with water bring to a boil. Remove from heat and set aside. Once cooled place in a spill proof container so mushrooms can rehydrate all day.

Dinnertime Prep: prepare the instant rice following package directions. Once rice is done set aside.

Add the mushroom mixture that has been soaking all day to a pot and bring to a boil, simmer for 10 minutes. Let mushroom mixture sit and continue to soften (rehydrate) as you prepare the rest of the dish.

Peel and chop the sweet potato into ½ inch cubes. In a large fry pan heat the oil on medium flame until oil is hot. Add the sweet potatoes and fry about 15 minutes, browning and flipping about every 5 minutes to cook and keep it from burning.

While potatoes cook, strain the mushroom mixture, press to remove excess water and set aside. Once the mushroom mixture is cool enough to touch chop (if needed) the mushrooms into smaller pieces.

When potatoes are almost done add the mushroom mixture, the cooked rice, the soy sauce, and the ginger to the large fry pan and stir.

In a separate bowl mix ova-easy eggs, dry whole milk powder and water, stir to remove lumps. Pour the egg mixture over the rice, mushrooms and sweet potatoes mixture in the large fry pan. Cook for a minute or so (if you have people in your group that do not eat eggs then cook the eggs in a separate pan to serve on side).

Prepare Tamarindo Sauce: in a separate bowl mix the True Lime, brown sugar and water. Pour the sauce over the mixture in the large fry pan, stir gently, and reheat if needed.

*any dried mushroom can be used and if you have a home dehydrator – dry your favorite mushroom!

*Notes for Future Reference. This recipe is especially good for playing around with, as many people have their favorite ingredients for making fried rice, just use my recipe as a rough guideline to create your unique fried rice recipe.

_____

_____

_____

_____

_____

_____

_____

Marley's South of the Border Burritos

In 1996 I signed up for a 6-day backpacking trip lead by Bob and Susan Marley to Rainbow Bridge, Utah. By that time, they already had over a decade of experience packing food for large-group, extended trips. Susan was the primary contributor to their extensive database of backpacking and rafting recipes. This dynamic duo was my inspiration for a new way of thinking about the camp kitchen.

This is one of their rafting recipes which I have tweaked a little. The cooking time and the amount of water required for the instant rice and refried beans will depend on the brand. Read the directions on the box carefully before preparing.

4 Servings

> 1 (6 ¾ ounce) package Rice-A-Roni Spanish Rice
>
> 2 tablespoons stick margarine
>
> 4 ½ ounces canned stewed tomato, diced
>
> 1 (6 ounce) package instant green chili refried beans (Mexicali Rose Brand)
>
> 2 tablespoons dried minced onion
>
> 4 ounces canned green chilies, diced
>
> 8 ounces cheese, grated (canned Bega Brand or Kraft Parmesan)*
>
> 8 burrito sized flour tortillas or make homemade Naan (see Side Dishes recipes)

½ cup salsa of your choice

4 ounces canned jalapeno peppers, sliced

½ cabbage head, small, thinly sliced

Spanish Rice: follow the directions on the Rice-A-Roni box. In a large skillet, combine rice and margarine. Sauté over medium heat until rice is golden brown, stirring frequently. Slowly stir in water, special seasonings and diced tomatoes, bring to a boil. Cover and reduce heat to low. Simmer 15 to 20 minutes or until rice is tender.

Instant Refried Beans: following the directions on the Instant Refried Beans package: bring beans and water for beans to a boil. Add the minced onions. Stir and simmer for 5 minutes on high, stirring occasionally to keep from sticking. Adjust beans with more water or longer cooking time until they are the consistency desired. Stir in the diced green chilies. Let sit 5 minutes.

Reheat rice and beans as needed. Heat tortillas over flame. Serve buffet style with tortillas, cheese, chilies and thin sliced cabbage. To turn up the heat add jalapeno peppers!

*Cheeses: canned cheese is an option I like – Really, it is great! Bega is the brand I like, so much so, that I keep it stocked in my kitchen at home. Canned cheese can be ordered online, see the Recipe Ingredients Notes section for ordering information. Also, for another cheese, try aged parmesan; I have had fresh aged parmesan cheese last for weeks without a cooler. But I often use Kraft brand dried parmesan cheese in recipes because it lasts a long time, even without refrigeration.

Vegetarian Tacos for Nomads

On occasion I seem to inspire other people into creating their own no coolers version of a favorite home or camping recipe. This recipe is an example.

I was surprised and delighted when my husband, Neil whom is a fabulous and creative cook, decided to take my commonly made recipe for fresh vegetarian tacos and experimented with it, creating his own no coolers version.

My home version uses all fresh items (onion, carrots, peppers, chili and in the home kitchen I add potatoes). Neil substituted the fresh items with dried ingredients and added taco-flavored TVP for the protein, substance and flavor. He played around with this recipe for quite a while, eventually coming up with this tasty version that works perfectly for the third week of a no coolers type camping trip.

4 Servings or about 12 good-sized tacos

⅓ cup chopped dehydrated onions

¼ cup diced dehydrated carrots

3 tablespoons dried diced mixed peppers

⅔ cup water

1 cup taco flavored TVP*

2 packages taco seasoning (I like Lawry's Hot)

1 tablespoon Ancho Chile powder

3 cups water

Corn tortillas (or crunchy pre-cooked taco shells)

Oil, enough to fry tortillas

Can salsa

Cheese (canned Bega, shredded or Kraft parmesan cheese, see Ingredient Notes)

Cabbage, shredded

Prior Evening Prep: add dehydrated vegetables to ⅔ cup water and let stand overnight. If you prepare the vegetables on the day of serving tacos, the vegetables must rehydrate for at least 30 minutes.

Dinnertime Prep: bring 2 cups of water to boil. Stir in vegetable mix, simmer for 5 minutes. Add taco flavored TVP and simmer for 10 minutes. If too dry add a little water. Stir in 1 cup of water and seasoning mix and Ancho Chile powder. Simmer until liquid is absorbed, stirring frequently.

As filling cooks, fry up the tortillas into taco shells, lay fried shells onto a paper towel to absorb excess oil and set aside.

To Assemble Taco: place a bit of the vegetarian taco filling into a taco shell, sprinkle with cheese, lay a bit of cabbage beside filling and splash some salsa over everything inside the taco shell.

*TVP (Taco Flavored) – Texturized vegetable protein (TVP) is a "soy meat." The soy beans provide protein, fiber, vitamins, and calcium. TVP is low in fat and cholesterol and has few calories.

Potato Corn Chowder

Excellent on a cool evening.

4 Servings

2 (4.2 ounce) boxes Hungry Jack dehydrated shredded potatoes

⅓ cup dried mixed peppers (Harmony House)

2 cups freeze-dried corn

3 cups water

1 teaspoon sugar

1 teaspoon salt

Pinch black ground pepper

½ cup dry whole milk powder (NIDO)

Thickener:

3 tablespoons Ultra Gel

1 cup water for mixing Ultra Gel

Morning Prep: combine the potatoes and mixed peppers in a large pot. Pour boiling water over them, stir, bring back to a full boil and remove from heat and set aside. Once cooled, place in a secure container so it can soak all day without spilling.

Dinnertime Prep: drain the potatoes. Return the drained potatoes to the large pot, add the freeze-dried corn and 3 cups of water to the large pot. Cover pot and bring to a boil. Low simmer for 5 minutes. After 5 minutes of simmering potatoes add milk powder, sugar, salt, and pepper and stir to mix.

In a separate bowl combine the Ultra Gel with water. Blend with fork so there are no lumps and then add to chowder. This will thicken the chowder. If you prefer the chowder thinner (or would like a larger quantity of chowder) add additional water ½ cup at a time.

Reheat, let sit for a minute and serve with salt and pepper.

Variation: for the vegetarian that consumes seafood.

Clam Chowder

If your "vegetarian" group will eat seafood, modify the Potato Corn Chowder accordingly. Replace the corn with clams.

> 1 shallot or small onion, diced
>
> 1 tablespoon margarine or oil
>
> 1 or 2 cans clams

Basically, follow the recipe for the Potato Corn Chowder. But, in addition, during the **Dinnertime Prep** add diced fresh shallots or a small diced onion to a separate pan and sauté. Once potatoes are cooked add the sautéed onions to the pot. After 10 minutes of simmering potatoes add milk powder, sugar, salt, and pepper, a can or two of clams. During the thickening with the Ultra Gel, more flavor can be added by including the clam liquid alongside the water or in place of. Finally stir all together to reheat and serve.

SIDE DISHES ~ DAYS 13 TO 18

Days 13 to 18: Effortless & Carefree – use the following recipes during the third week of a long trip.

Fried Platanos

Surprisingly simple and tasty, I hope you will try it.

4 Servings

> 4 very ripe platanos* (plantains)
>
> 1 cup vegetable oil for frying
>
> Salt (optional)

In a frying pan, heat oil over medium heat.

Peel plantains and cut into 1/2-inch-thick slices. Add to the frying pan.

Cook on each side until golden brown, about 2-3 minutes. Remove from the oil into a plate covered with a paper towel to remove excess grease. Sprinkle with a little salt, if desired.

Serve warm as a side dish or appetizer.

*Platanos (plantain) are a common food in Spanish speaking countries. In fact, it is a staple in many parts of the world. Most USA grocery stores carry it.

If you are not familiar with plantains, they look like a large banana. Stores and Mercado's usually sell them green. For the best texture and flavor buy green, but let it completely ripen to a yellow with a few black spots before cooking.

Mexican Chayote

A tangy fresh chayote dish. Chayote is the wonder vegetable!

4 Servings

   2 tablespoons oil

   4 Chayote, peeled, seed removed, cut into ½ inch
   cubes

   2 shallots, chopped

   2 serrano chili peppers, seeds removed and
   chopped

   2 tablespoons True Lime

   ¼ cup water for True Lime

   Salt and pepper

In a large sauté pan, add oil and heat on medium high
heat. Add Chayote. Cook for about 15 minutes in a
single layer, stir every 2 minutes or so.

Add shallots and chili peppers. Cook for about 5
minutes. If sauté looks a little dry add a few
tablespoons of water. Sauté until water has absorbed.
Remove from heat.

Reconstitute the lime juice in a separate container. Mix
the True Lime with the water to make juice. Drizzle
about 1 tablespoon over the chayote, then taste. Add
more lime juice if desired, adjusting for your palate.
Mix well. Reheat as needed. Serve with the remaining
lime juice on the side. Salt and pepper to taste.

Spanish Rice for Nomads

This recipe is pretty close to traditional Spanish rice, which is made from lots of veggies and tomato juice. I have modified the fresh version into a recipe that works very well for the no coolers camp kitchen, even into the third week; with dehydrated veggies and fresh chayote (the wonder vegetable).

Note: I dehydrate the corn, carrots and peas at home for a cost savings and convenience. Many modern small counter top appliances have a fan and a very low heat setting for dehydrating. I use mine often.

4 Servings

¾ cups rice

2 tablespoons oil

1 (5.5 ounce) Spicy V-8 juice

½ teaspoon garlic powder

2 teaspoons mild chili powder – like Ancho*

½ teaspoon salt

1 tablespoon dried onion (diced or minced)

1 ¾ cups vegetable broth (or 1 ¾ cups water with 1 vegetable bouillon cubes)

3 tablespoons dehydrated corn*

2 tablespoons dehydrated carrots (chopped or diced)*

2 tablespoons dehydrated peas*

1 chayote, seed removed, peeled, and diced

Lightly brown rice in oil in large fry pan on med-high heat. Stir often to avoid sticking. Add tomato juice and cook for 5 minutes on low heat, stirring.

Stir in broth, garlic and chili powder, and salt, dried vegetables, and (optional) chayote. Continue cooking on medium heat.

When rice begins to boil, turn heat to low, cover and cook for about 20 minutes (add water if absorbed before 20 minutes).

Remove from heat and let rest for 5 minutes, fluff & serve.

*Ancho Chile Powder – Ancho chilies have a milder, sweeter flavor than the American style chili powder. Look for ancho chili powder in the "International" aisle of your supermarket or at a local Mexican market. Do not replace with regular chili powders, as the flavors are different. Ancho chili powder is made from dried Poblano peppers

*Dehydrated corn, carrots and peas are pretty easy to dry at home if you have a home dehydrator. Some of the newer counter top toaster ovens include a dehydrator function. I use my Cuisinart Digital AirFryer Toaster Oven for dehydrating small batches of vegetables and fruit. This counter tip appliance has a dehydrator setting. The lowest heat setting on this little counter top unit 130 degrees, which I have found to be a good temperature for dehydrating corn, carrots (chopped fine) and peas. I dehydrate them in separate batches not all together because each particular vegetable takes a different amount of time to dry.

Homemade Garlic Naan

This recipe yields a very soft, chewy naan; just the way I like it!

This is a good recipe if you want fresh bread late in a trip. Like a multi-week Grand Canyon trip, where by the third week you usually only have crackers, stale bread or bread loaded with preservatives left.

This may be one of the most time consuming and difficult recipes in this cookbook, which does not particularly fit with the ease of the other recipes intended to be used in the third week, but it is so nice to have fresh bread on the last week of a multi-week trip that I believe the hard work may be worth it.

Try this recipe on that last week if you desire fresh bread. In reality, it will work at any point in a trip.

I suggest you try it out at home first; have a trial run before preparing in the woods of the camp kitchen.

Makes 8 pieces naan

> 1 ½ cups warm water
>
> 1 tablespoon sugar
>
> 2 teaspoons active dry yeast
>
> 1 teaspoon salt
>
> 3 cups flour, plus a few tablespoons for dusting the workspace
>
> 6 cloves garlic
>
> 6 tablespoons stick margarine

Combine warm water, sugar, and yeast in a bowl. Let stand for 5 minutes until foamy.

Add salt and flour to the yeast water. Mix thoroughly. Knead dough on a floured workspace about 20 times and form into a tight ball. Put dough in a well-oiled bowl and cover with a damp towel. Put in a warm place to rise for 30-45 minutes. The dough won't rise much, but it doesn't need to.

Mince garlic and sauté in margarine for a few minutes.

Turn dough out onto a floured workspace. Divide dough into 8 pieces. If I were to make this at home, I would use a rolling pin, but while camping one can improvise. A Nalgene bottle will work in place of a rolling pin. Wash and completely dry the bottle. Using the bottle as a rolling pin flatten dough to about 1/8" thick (like a tortilla).

Place a little bit of margarine in a frying pan (not necessary but if you have some spray oil, that works well). Cook each naan over a medium high flame for 2 minutes or so on each side. If you do not have a timer then cook until bubbles form and is slightly browned one each side. You want the pan to be hot enough that the bread forms bubbles as they cook, but not so hot that it burns.

As each piece of bread finishes cooking, brush naan with a bit of the garlic margarine and stack on plate until all are cooked. When all are done serve the plate of naan to your guests.

Creamed Chayote

Chayote is a type of squash native to the Americas. It is a small, hard and mild flavored squash that retains a bit of firmness even when cooked.

4 Servings

> 3 chayote
>
> 1 tablespoon stick margarine
>
> 1 tablespoon flour
>
> 4 tablespoons dry whole milk powder (NIDO)
>
> 1 cup water
>
> Salt and pepper to taste

Peel, seed and slice two chayote.

The easiest way to prepare this versatile vegetable for this recipe is to cut each chayote into quarters, then slice the quarters into six or eight wedges (depending on size of chayote) then peel and deseed. Cut each wedge into three pieces.

Place chayote's pieces in a pan, cover with water and boil for about 8 minutes. Cook until they are soft to the bite, but still green in color. Drain and set aside.

Reconstitute the milk powder. To make the white sauce, melt margarine in a pan. Stir in the flour to make a paste. Slowly add the reconstituted milk and constantly stir over medium to low heat until thickened, bubbling, and there are no more lumps.

Add the drained chayote to white sauce. Salt and pepper to taste.

DESSERTS ~ DAYS 13 TO 18

Days 13 to 18: Effortless & Carefree – use the following recipes during the third week of a long trip.

Chocolate Chia Pudding

This is a very healthy alternative to traditional pudding. This takes a few hours though, so start as soon as your camp kitchen is set-up when you pull into camp.

You may have to play around with this recipe a bit to find the perfect ratio of chia seed to reconstituted milk, as not all chia seed brands are the same. Some thicken up quicker and better than others. I do believe that chia freshness also plays a part.

4 Servings

> 4 tablespoons dry whole milk powder (NIDO)
>
> 1 ½ cups water (almond or rice milk can be substituted)
>
> ⅓ cup chia seeds
>
> ¼ cup unsweetened cocoa powder
>
> ¼ cup sugar (maple syrup or honey can be substituted)
>
> ¼ teaspoon salt

Add all ingredients to a mixing bowl and whisk vigorously to combine.

Let rest for at least 2 hours. After a few hours it will become "pudding"

Alternative prep method. Make it in the morning and let set all day, then serve that evening for dessert.

Rum Balls

One of my favorite holiday treats, but good in the camp kitchen any time of year!

Makes About 20 Balls

Balls

> ½ cup finely chopped walnuts or pecans
>
> 1 cup finely crushed vanilla wafers (Nilla Vanilla Wafer type)
>
> ¾ cup powdered sugar
>
> 1 tablespoon cocoa powder
>
> ¼ teaspoon ground allspice
>
> ¼ cup dark rum
>
> 1 tablespoon honey or light corn syrup (Karo Syrup)

Coating

> ½ cup finely chopped vanilla wafers

At Home Prep: in a food processor first finely chop the walnuts and then separately process the 1 ½ cups of vanilla wafers. Place the chopped nuts and only 1 cup of the chopped wafers in a bag. Place the remaining ½ cup of chopped vanilla wafers in a different gallon size bag.

Dinnertime Prep: in a large bowl, mix together ¾ cup of the confectioners' sugar, the cocoa powder and allspice. Stir in the rum and honey. Stir in the 1 cup of vanilla wafers and the chopped nuts then mix well.

Scoop out about ½ tablespoon portion sizes of the chocolate mixture and roll into small balls. Using your hands, roll the balls in the baggie full of ½ cup of chopped vanilla wafers, coating evenly. Make one at a time rolling in the cookie crumbs, remove from bag and set on plate to serve. If there are any left-over store in the bag of crushed cookie crumbs, preventing them from sticking together.

Mud Cookies

Measure and have ready all of the ingredients before starting to prepare because they may set-up fast after coming to a boil.

Yields about a dozen tablespoon sized cookies.

> 1 tablespoon dry whole milk powder (NIDO)
>
> ¼ cup water for milk
>
> 1 cup sugar
>
> ½ stick margarine (¼ cup)
>
> ¼ cup peanut butter
>
> 1 ½ cup quick oats
>
> 1 ½ tablespoon cocoa
>
> ½ tablespoon vanilla

Reconstitute milk by adding powdered milk to the ¼ cup water.

In largish pan combine the sugar, reconstituted milk, margarine and cocoa; bring to a boil over medium flame, turn flame to low and boil for 5 minutes. Watch and stir often so it does not boil over or burn. As mixture cooks prepare a surface for the cookies to be dropped onto.

Remove from heat and quickly stir in the oats, peanut butter and vanilla. Mix thoroughly and drop by heaping tablespoon onto waxed paper.

If mixture starts to harden before you are through, add a few drops of milk or water, re-stir and finish dropping onto waxed paper.

168

Chocolate PB Medjools

Dates are considered the oldest cultivated fruit in the world. Fossil evidence shows that date palms lived 50 million years ago. The fruit of the date palm has been cultivated for about 6,000 years in the Middle East. Dates are a staple part of many cultures' diets because of their nutritional value and easy portability.

Serves 4

> 8 extra-large Medjool Dates*
>
> 2 tablespoons peanut butter
>
> 1 tablespoon instant milk powder
>
> ¾ tablespoon brown sugar
>
> 2 tablespoons Nutella
>
> 8 pecan halves

Prepare dates first. Split dates lengthwise to remove seed but do not cut completely in half because they will be stuffed, set aside.

Prepare filling. Mix the peanut butter, milk powder and brown sugar, set aside.

Fill one half of date with about 1 teaspoon of peanut butter filling and fill the other half of the date with about ¼ teaspoon of Nutella. Partially close each date and top with a pecan half.

For serving presentation, lay them out on a plate in a pleasing pattern and serve.

*Medjool Dates are my favorite variety because of the flavor and large size.

Chocolate Coconut Balls

So good, so simple!

4 Servings about 16 balls

   ⅔ cups peanut butter

   1½ teaspoons vanilla extract

   ¼ cup cocoa powder

   1 cup sweetened shredded coconut

   ¼ cup raisins

   ½ cup powdered sugar + enough to roll balls in
   (about ¾ cup total)

In a large mixing bowl, combine the peanut butter,
vanilla extract, coconut flakes, cocoa, raisins and ½ cup
powdered sugar and stir until well combined.

Scoop batter into 1-inch round balls and roll in
powdered sugar, set on plate to serve.

Store in the left-over powdered sugar.

Snip, snap, that's that – I hope you liked it!

ABOUT THE AUTHOR

Lacey is a veteran of the outdoors, having guided river rafters and backpackers all over the western United States, Mexico and Peru. Her decades of experience, both rafting and backpacking, provide her with a unique perspective on meal planning and allow her to create scrumptious meals that are low in bulk, lightweight, and nonperishable. The recipes provided here are only a sampling of the hundreds of meal ideas she has developed over the years. She is constantly refining and adding to her catalog of recipes in response to the inspiration, "Hey that could work well in the no coolers camp kitchen." A few years ago, she began compiling her vegetarian recipes that work without refrigeration/coolers. The result was the Camp Without Coolers Vegetarian series of books.

A few articles have been written about Lacey; one was published in the American Whitewater Journal titled, "Lacey Anderson. Whitewater Maven." NRS has published a couple of biographical sketches about Lacey in their e-newsletter (Duct Tape Diaries), one article is titled, "Life of a River Gypsy." The NGO Paddling with Purpose did an interview with Lacey titled, "Fiercely Independent River Gypsy." You can find out more about Lacey, more about camp cooking, and keep up with her latest exploits on her website at www.nocoolers.com.

Intrigued by her lifestyle? Think you might want to lead that lifestyle? After reading the following Canoe & Kayak article written by the talented journalist Tyler Williams, you might change your mind.

When Lacey Anderson was held captive by an angry mob in farthest Guatemala, she came to a stunning epiphany. "I realized," she recalls, "that this could be my last day." For Lacey, the cold realization of mortality came with more irony than most. Lacey grew up in Southern California as a "wild child," she says; reared through the foggy lens of addiction, growing into another high school dropout. Fortunately, an innate connection with nature provided some peace. She read how-to books on camping and took her first backpacking trip at sixteen. Nature's solace led her back to school where she earned a GED and a teaching degree, and eventually her own classroom of sixth graders. She had two daughters. Life went on.

Then, Lacey took a raft trip on the South Fork of the American. Her guide was female, and Lacey thought, "I can do this." A part time guiding career followed, both on rivers and trails, but it wasn't until her two daughters were grown and she tired of education's bureaucracy that Lacey redoubled her river interests and made it her life. Since 2009, Anderson has lived primarily out of her tricked-out Toyota camper truck, following runoff seasons from Idaho's snowmelt to Mexico's monsoon. In the extra cab of her truck rides a custom built cataraft, perfect for the small and obscure rivers Anderson seeks.

Lacey's travels crossed paths with a kayak explorer a couple years ago, and the two have since completed over two dozen multi-day rivers throughout Mexico, from Sonora's Aros to Oaxaca's Atoyac. Several were first descents, not an endeavor normally suited to bulky rafts, but Anderson's extra small cataraft *makes portaging a relative breeze, and she knows how to go light.*

Several years ago, while running support for kayakers on the Middle Fork of the Salmon (a river she regularly guides), Lacey organized impeccably gourmet meals without the use of a cooler. Her well-fed paddlers insisted that she publish the magic menu, and thus came Camp Without Coolers, a guide to tasty river meals attainable without burdensome blocks of ice.

Her backpack boating style has helped Lacey go deep in search of jungle rivers like Guatemala's revered Copon, where her river-liberating film party was mistaken for corporate dam meddlers, and held at machete point while villagers threatened live immolation as punishment. Brave negotiations from the river parties' bravest Guatemalan companion Max B. negotiated their release, and she knew it wasn't her "last day," after all. It was just another life lesson, one she'll hopefully not have to employ on Peru's Maranon, a storied Amazon source river that Lacey will row next winter. It's a long way from her Southern California roots, but for Lacey Anderson, maturing river gypsy, it's home.

If you are interested in the quality, lightweight boating equipment that Lacey uses, look-up go light outdoors website for information about light weight catarafts, frames, oars and more www.golightoutdoors.com

If you enjoyed this article you can read more, contact Lacey or simply follow along at her no coolers website www.nocoolers.com

ADDITIONAL TITLES

I have a 3-booklet series of this cookbook just in case people are interested in only a particular week from this book. These booklets are titled: **Fresh and Healthy**, **Quick and Easy** and **The Nomad**.

There is even a No Cooking philosophy "cookbook". Yup! I said <u>No Cooking!</u> Thus, no cooler, <u>no stove</u>, <u>no fuel</u>, and <u>no fire</u> which means no coals and ashes to pack out or deal with! It is available in both paperback and as an eBook titled, **Camp Without Coolers or Stoves ~ Tasty Meals with Absolutely NO COOKING!**

Not a vegetarian? Perhaps you would be interested in the original CWC title, **Camp Cooking WITHOUT Coolers II ~ Blueprint for using nonperishable food.** This cookbook includes an extensive 7-day meal plan using only nonperishable ingredients. And yes, many of the recipes have animal protein.

WEBSITE / CONTACT

Please feel free to contact me at www.nocoolers.com On the website you will find tips on how to plan, pack, and prepare delicious food on multi-day outings using no coolers techniques. Also, on the website is a button to join my bi-annual newsletter with opportunities for discounted sales, eBooks and more!

THANK YOU

I am so thankful for all the amazing, positive feedback that my series of cookbooks has gotten. It's very humbling and encouraging.

174

If you like the book or found it helpful ... and if you'd be willing to spare just two or three minutes...please share your review of the cookbook on Amazon.

Here's how:

1. Go to the cookbook purchase page on Amazon
2. Click. Write a customer review in the Customer Review section.
3. Add text, photos, or videos and click Submit.

Thank you so much! This helps me get the book into as many hands as possible and help others discover the simplicity and benefits of the Camp Without Cooler philosophy!

I really appreciate all your support, you all rock!

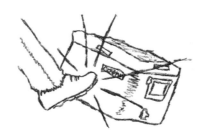

Kick the Cooler Habit!

Made in the USA
Las Vegas, NV
05 June 2022

49834174R00105